# Practically Perfect

# Practically Perfect

## Life Lessons from Mary Poppins

# KATY BRAND

ONE PLACE. MANY STORIES

HQ
An imprint of HarperCollins*Publishers* Ltd
1 London Bridge Street
London SE1 9GF

This edition 2020

1
First published in Great Britain by
HQ, an imprint of HarperCollins*Publishers* Ltd 2020

HB ISBN: 978-0-00-840070-5
TPB ISBN: 978-0-00-840071-2

Typeset by Type-it AS, Norway

Printed and bound in Great Britain by
CPI Group (UK) Ltd, Croydon, CR0 4YY

This book provides an analysis of the Walt Disney film *Mary Poppins* (1964),
including by reference to the books by P.L. Travers that the film dramatises.

In memory of
Violet Brand, MBE
(1929–2020)

# Contents

# Introduction

*Mary Poppins* was my favourite film as a child. I was captivated by the songs, the dancing chimney sweeps, the magic. I loved the idea that you could have a day out inside a pavement painting or a tea party on the ceiling. And I was enthralled by the mysterious nanny herself, of course. I liked the crispness of *Mary Poppins*, the pace, the magical otherness of it and the comfort of an old London I had never known for myself but which somehow felt like home. There were the kindly eccentrics laughing their way through life and the notion that a pair of young children could go missing in a city-centre park and be delivered home by the friendly and familiar local bobby before anyone really had time to panic.

The way I felt after watching *Mary Poppins* at ten years old was 'invincible'. I thought I could achieve anything with a bit of stiff resolve and a perky attitude. It always made me want to go upstairs and tidy my room. I felt aflutter with possibilities. A small clear-up would then turn into a total clear-out and I would end up turning all the drawers out, cleaning shelves, pulling furniture away from the wall to see what was behind. Bags of rubbish would accumulate and, when it was done, I would sit on the bed in wonder, gazing at the

3

perfect order in front of me. I'd end up doing my homework too, just to prolong the feeling of virtue. Hell, sometimes I even polished my shoes. I resolved that I would be just like Mary Poppins when I was older – I would run a tight ship, never panic or flap about, and keep a close eye on my own personal care.

Watching the film back as an adult, I have realised that one of the things that I was responding to, which now speaks to me even more loudly, is that Mary Poppins really couldn't care less about your expectations, your sense of order and rectitude or the perceived societal conventions of the day. She's here to deliver deeper truths in the manner that she sees fit, whilst appearing immaculately turned out at all times and maintaining constant poise. It's utterly thrilling.

For me, *Mary Poppins* is a story about taking practical steps towards happiness. It is about setting boundaries and then upholding those boundaries for a better life. It's about deciding how you want your life to be and then taking action to make it happen. Even if all that means is a little tidy-up, it's still a good start.

This has been my small revelation, courtesy of *Mary Poppins* – I can talk, and think, and imagine all I like, and worlds will be built in my mind; I can engage in necessary introspection and let it tip into indulgent navel gazing from time to time. I can spend all morning saying, 'I'm going for a run,' and then decide at lunchtime it's too late in the day now and I'll go tomorrow, then spend some more time analysing my emotions to establish why I didn't go for that run. But until I actually do something practical, and tangible, nothing will change. This, as I have found, is the 'Poppins Doctrine' – that recognising a need to change and then taking practical action is what leads to greater happiness. But you must make a start. You could even say, 'Well begun is half done.'

Just recently, Mary Poppins has started to feel like the answer to a question I have been reaching for but not quite grasping; the solution to a problem I can feel but can't quite define. We sit at our desks but don't feel productive – why? We talk about healthy food endlessly but still reach for the crisps – why? We feel tired all the time but we won't go to bed early – why? I can run up my own list of excuses as long as your arm, and I frequently do. I have got into the habit of excusing myself for anything I don't feel like doing. But as I watched *Mary Poppins*, I started to blush as I imagined the look on her face while I whined at her about my foot being a bit sore, or how I can't write today because I've spent all morning googling my chakras and now I'm out of time, or I couldn't sleep because I was up until 2am arguing with a stranger on Twitter about how to make a proper carbonara.

She would fix me with that glinty, flinty look of hers and I would crumple in a heap of shame. *Mary Poppins* may be an old film, but it has a fresh message. I think Mary's still got something to teach us. Her lessons have been lost a little and bringing them back wouldn't do us any harm at all.

The film *Mary Poppins* was released by Walt Disney in 1964 and was an immediate success. It takes themes such as parental neglect, women's rights, poverty, financial power, toxic masculinity, work/ life balance, boundaries and the importance of holidays, and brings them all together in a confection as light as a posh meringue with enough chewy stuff in the middle to make to feel you've really eaten something proper. It's entertaining, joyful, moving and satisfying. It's family entertainment for grown-ups, which is of course the best kind. And it has some of the greatest songs ever written in the history of film. Or indeed songwriting, full stop.

Mary Poppins the character, though, was brought to life some three decades before that by a woman called Helen Lyndon Goff, writing under the name Pamela L Travers. *Mary Poppins*, the first of eight books she would write about Mary, was published in 1934 and told the story of a super-cocky, magical nanny who comes to look after the children of Mr and Mrs Banks of Cherry Tree Lane, London.

Travers continued writing books about Mary Poppins until 1988 but none lived up to the spiky, saucy first and, ultimately, they were all eclipsed (at least in terms of mainstream success) by Disney's celluloid creation. As fans of the books will know, Disney's Poppins was different to Travers' Poppins in some respects – Travers' creation was plain rather than pretty, she was often brusque and dismissive of the children and she wasn't much interested in romancing chimney sweeps. She was more singular, perhaps, more alone. The film rather swept these nuances away in favour of a character who was more conventionally appealing.

Although it is sad to lose a little of the original vision of the author and creator, it also shows the power of the genius of Disney. He didn't take on *Mary Poppins* out of some cynical, money-making exploitation of the work of another. He loved the books as much as his two daughters did. Disney's desire to make the movie of *Mary Poppins* was first ignited around Christmas of 1944, when he heard eleven-year-old Diane laughing with joy at the original 1934 book. She begged her father to get the rights for his animation company.

He tried and tried. For the best part of twenty years, Disney pursued Travers, but she wouldn't budge. Until finally, in 1959, she changed her mind. Or had it changed for her by a new American lawyer and an offer she couldn't refuse. A hundred thousand dollars was on the table, plus a percentage of the profits. At this point, Travers was feeling hard up and worried about the future. She signed the deal. By the time the film finally came out, Diane Disney was in her thirties.

Did Travers regret it? Probably. It was certainly bittersweet for her, though she enjoyed the lifetime financial security it brought her. The pre-production, filming and release of *Mary Poppins* were all fraught with tension, as Travers tried to keep control of her creation. She had script approval as part of the deal and was determined it would not become a cartoon. Travers and Disney had what she later described as an 'uneasy wedlock'. But I can't regret her decision to sell, because though the books are dark, unusual, original and funny, the film is just sheer, effervescent delight from start to finish.

It was Julie Andrews's first Hollywood film and it won her an Oscar. It was as if she was made to play Poppins – a cookie-cutter perfect woman, but with a glint in her eye you could cut diamonds with. And the rest of the cast were equally perfect: Dick Van Dyke, David Tomlinson, Glynis Johns all shine and twinkle through every moment. It's a Sunday-afternoon film for the ages. It will get you through any rainy day. Or in my experience, any hangover.

Disney was rightly proud of his creation. He used cutting-edge technology, including special cameras of his own design and manufacture, to make the sequences involving a mix of live action and animation, splicing film between painted pieces of glass and then refilming them as composite plates. Nobody else in the world had access to anything similar because Disney had invented it himself.

In her autobiography, *Home Work*, Julie Andrews writes of the difficulty in filming in a medium that was new to everyone. They would rehearse the dance sequences for songs like 'Step in Time' for hours in a baking hot marquee on the Disney lot at Burbank, California, unaware that they would ultimately be seen to be dancing on staircases made of smoke, or jumping down narrow chimney pots only to appear on a roof next door. Andrews describes once being 'strapped to a pole on a lazy Susan and whipped around like a spinning top', and 'hanging from the rafters on wires'. The 'Spoonful of Sugar' nursery scene was shot in reverse: wires pulled drawers open and unfolded clothes, and then the film was run backwards to show the messy room tidying itself up on Mary Poppins' command.

People were amazed when they saw it in cinemas – nobody had ever seen anything like this before. The profits were used to fund the creation of Disney World, following the success of Disneyland – another project that the visionary Walt had been determined to finish, even painting backdrops and rides himself alongside workers who carried on through the night to be ready in time for the official opening. He was dogged, determined and always finding new and creative ways to show what he could do. He was not an easy man, and his decisions were not always popular. But he would not stop for anyone. He would not explain himself. He did what he thought was right and necessary to achieve the results he desired. No wonder he loved Mary Poppins. In this respect at least, they were very similar.

In the process of researching this book and trying to get to grips with what makes this film from 1964 feel both enchanting and still relevant, I have spoken to some friends and fans and included what they told me. One thing that comes up repeatedly is that it is comforting.

We return to the film again and again to imbibe that feeling that everything will be all right in the end. Who could fail to be uplifted by Julie Andrews whistling a duet with an improbably large animatronic robin? And then of course there are the visuals. We have become so accustomed to the use of CGI in films, with the aim of making impossible things look real. But there is something so appealing about the mouth-watering painted backdrops of Edwardian London. The crisp and colourful costumes are delightful; the glorious technicolour of it all is so much better than anything more photo-realistic.

Lots of people told me how much they have enjoyed – or are looking forward to – sharing it with their own children, even though it is essentially a film about parents getting everything wrong. There is something so compelling about that childlike desire for order to emerge out of the chaos of family life, for a kind stranger to arrive and make everything better – someone who knows what they're doing and will show us where we are going wrong. It's an idea that appeals to almost everyone; you don't have to have had an especially traumatic childhood to get it, although interestingly both P L Travers and Walt Disney had a difficult time when they were young. Bearing in mind what we know of Travers, it's hard to imagine that these two would have shared their experiences with one another directly, but it seems that something communicated itself across the divide, expressed, as it so often is, via the medium of story.

Something that I love about Mary Poppins is her lack of emotional need. She seems entirely self-sufficient, to the point of arrogance at times, and nothing seems to shame her. I find it intoxicating, and I am not alone in this. Emma Thompson, who played Travers brilliantly and sensitively in the film *Saving Mr Banks* opposite Tom Hanks as Walt Disney, agrees:

*'I think for women particularly her special power is absolutely her lack of emotional neediness. It's what we all want – well, I do anyway. I feel very needy emotionally – perhaps I am, perhaps I am not, but I feel it. Any character who is truly self-sufficient without being aloof and cut off is so attractive to me. Mary Poppins doesn't need the children to love her. She doesn't need anything. But she is nonetheless fully engaged and present.'*

What an immense power to hold. It is remarkable and, as Emma says, so attractive. Of course, it is unrealistic to expect or demand the same from any real human, especially any mother, or indeed parent. We are only human – we have needs, and weaknesses, and vulnerabilities and, though we may try to hide them from ourselves and our children, they always leak out. Children can sense it a mile off and will often recoil from extremely needy people, or 'thirsty' people as I believe it's now called by those with super-active Instagram accounts who know what on earth TikTok is. It's a relief and an inspiration to watch a woman like Poppins go about her business without apology or explanation, without shame or the need for approval. I'm just going to say it: it's sexy.

In fact, lots of people seem to find Mary Poppins a bit sexy. It's easy when Julie Andrews is both naughty and nice. Bert certainly seems to think so. Of course, it's not front and centre, and strike me down for saying it, but there is a kind of undeniable sex appeal to the whole film. It's partly what makes it endure and allows it to be appealing to adults. Mrs Banks looks like she doesn't mind a little bit of "ow's yer father', as Bert might say, and ooh Bert, yes, he's got that troubadour free spirit thing going on. Anyone who likes their men a bit buttoned up could imagine helping Mr Banks relax a little. Ellen and Cook may hold a bit more of a niche appeal but there's plenty who would love a rummage with a buxom servant after the master's gone upstairs – just ask Julian Fellowes, he's made a career out of writing it.

Is this a shocking suggestion? Well, not if a recent (though not entirely scientific) survey on Twitter (conducted by me, again, emphatically not a scientist) is anything to go by. When I asked if it was odd to have a little crush on Bert, I was engulfed with responses about the various objects of desire to be found in *Mary Poppins*. So if I'm outrageous, I'm certainly not outrageous by myself. A fleeting but appropriate sense of the adult world and good chemistry between the actors are essential to the success of any film aimed at children. They soak it all up. They sense the reality and the tension, and part of that tension is attraction. It's a necessary ingredient because it has a flash of danger about it. Most fairy tales begin or end with a kiss.

And continuing with adult themes, Mary Poppins has a political dimension too, with the deliberate subverting of the capitalist system and Poppins herself pushing a more radical agenda on the children than the one their father expects them to accept. Bert has declined to join in with the English middle-class obsession with conformity, investment, property ownership, family life and a steady job and is by far the happiest person in the film. And of course, there's the suffragettes and female power more generally, which is the motor that keeps the entire narrative running. What are the roles for each of us in society? What do we owe each other? What do we owe ourselves?

To be free, to be self-sufficient, to have and maintain personal boundaries, to not indulge our weaknesses, to help those in need and care for our loved ones in a real and present way and, above all, to be practical, positive and well-turned out in the face of any hardship and upheaval, taking action where required without procrastinating or whinging – that's the path to being Practically Perfect. That's the Poppins Doctrine. To put our best foot forward. To have some self-respect. To take positive action. These are the messages Mary Poppins wishes to impart to the Banks family, but also to us, the viewer. I feel I could do with a dose of her medicine from time to time, sweetened with a spoonful of sugar.

# Chapter 1

# Supercalifragilisticexpialidocious

*H*ow do you like your heroines? I look back at those I have latched onto over the course of my life and see one common thread: practicality. As a child, I loved Enid Blyton's good sense girls, whether that was George from the Famous Five, who I identified with enormously – Blyton's personal politics may have been seriously dubious, but she created a gender-fluid character long before time – and Darrell Rivers, who starred in her boarding school series, Malory Towers. These were girls who advised you should get back on the horse every time you fell off and not cry if you scraped your knee. They had little patience for 'girly nonsense'.

Darrell Rivers was the absolute epitome of these practical, jolly, sensible girls – just a 'good egg'. She was reliable, loyal and capable. When she made a mistake (a big plot point is her famously hot temper) she immediately resolved to sort it out, rather than expecting someone else to help her – though she often came up with schemes and plans to help her friends. Her arch nemesis was a girl called Gwendoline who was spoiled by her rich parents and always made a big fuss when she was dropped off at school for the new term. 'Making a fuss' is a crime beyond compare for Enid Blyton's heroines. Good eggs accept their lot, make the best of it and they never, ever make a fuss.

I joined the Brownies when I was eight, partly because everyone else I knew did and partly because I liked being tested on my ability to make afternoon tea (complete with doily) for a local old lady and then being given a badge for it. I wanted to join in and I wanted to conform, to some extent. I think most children do – we want to be the same as everyone else until the age of around thirteen, when we suddenly want to be different from everyone else, thereby remaining the same as everyone else. The ultimate irony of teenage-hood. Although there are always some cool outliers – for example, a girl I was friends with around that time joined a group called the Woodcraft Folk because, as she somewhat precociously informed me, 'The Brownies are a paramilitary organisation,' or, at least, that's what her dad said.

Anyway, though I could never achieve that level of cool anti-establishmentarianism, it seems a hint of teenage rebellion also came early to me, as my time in the Brownies ended somewhat disastrously after a couple of years when I was asked to leave for 'treating it as a fashion show'. Trust me when I say I have never treated anything as a fashion show in my life, not even when I was at an actual fashion show – a friendly designer let me film myself walking down the catwalk dressed as Kate Moss for my comedy website. That is as close as I have ever got to a fashion show, and I still couldn't take it seriously.

No, what they meant was that I didn't want to wear long socks and would roll them down to my ankles. This, it seems, was the hill

I was willing to die on. My legs are stumpy. I cannot carry off a long sock with knee-length brown skirt. I knew this, even at ten years old. It remains the case. And I was willing to forgo all the fun and conformity of being a Brownie for the sake of a more flattering sock. Also, Tawny Owl simply didn't like me. So I was gone.

But I still wanted to learn some skills; I wanted to be a sensible, reliable sort you could count on to have a ten-pence piece and a length of string in her pocket in an emergency. And so, in the spirit of being a 'good egg' – as I still very much wanted to be in case I ever met Darrell Rivers in real life – I put it behind me and joined the Girl Guides. But again it was not to be.

I was thirteen by now and a bit too old and cynical; I took to Sellotaping my pathetic three badges to my uniform instead of sewing them on, and generally 'subverting the nature of the organisation', as the inevitable letter home read. I couldn't do it. I tried, but something else was bubbling up in me that didn't seem welcome there. A sort of sense of the absurdity of it all. Well, the two leaders voluntarily called themselves Pooh and Piglet. I don't see how anyone could fail to subvert the nature of that. A grown woman shouting, 'Oh, Pooh! Where are you?' in a game of woodland hide and seek is not a way to control unruly teenage girls.

I did want to join in and be good, though. I wasn't naturally a troublemaker. It's just that inevitably something would strike me as funny and I couldn't hold it inside. I loved to laugh. Yes, that's right – loud, and long, and clear. And it would often get the better of me. I once had the school librarian and the headmaster standing over me, trying to send me out of the library for bad behaviour, while I tried to indicate that I was paralysed with mirth and would leave as soon as I could stop laughing. What an absolute prat.

Later in life, I discovered Jackie Collins (hard-nosed bitches who gave as good as they got) and Jilly Cooper (hard-shagging bitches who gave as good as they got). All these female characters that I looked up to were essentially the same – and yes, that is a direct line from Blyton to Collins that I'm drawing – they got on with things, they didn't complain and they didn't explain. If life gets dirty, roll up your sleeves, don't indulge in sentiment, and if a box of lemons comes your way, well, you know what to do. Robust, jolly-hockey-sticks Darrell Rivers has more in common with the ball-breaking and impossibly glamorous Lucky Santangelo than we might think.

And in amongst all this is Mary Poppins. I loved *Mary Poppins*, both in book form and on film. The smash hit 1964 film is the first experience most have of Poppins, as it was mine. And I loved it. Between the ages of eight and ten, when asked what I would like to do for my birthday, I would request two things: I wanted macaroni cheese for tea and afterwards I wanted to watch *Mary Poppins*. My mum would say, 'Are you *sure* that's all you want to do?' and I would nod enthusiastically. I was quite sure. This happened for three consecutive birthdays and I was very happy about it. (Then I discovered *Dirty Dancing* which, as you may know because I've hardly kept it a secret, rather took over from that point on.)

Part of the joy of watching *Mary Poppins* as a child is the thrill of her unshakeable confidence. She is fully in control at all times, even as chaos threatens and, what's more, she's cocky with it. This is one of my most striking memories – her attitude. She looks so prim and proper, but underneath it all she is anarchy made flesh. She tears up the rule book with a butter wouldn't melt expression. She's both safe and dangerous at the same time.

You can ask people, and I have, whether they think *Mary Poppins* is a story about a nanny or a witch. Most, if you don't give them too long to think, will almost immediately say 'nanny', then pause, furrow their brow a little and follow up with, 'But hold on . . .' Because this is the central mystery: who is Mary Poppins? Where did she come from? And then, where does she go? Not a question the film even attempts to answer and it would probably get a sharp look from Poppins herself for immense impertinence if it did. Instead, she floats into the Banks family's life and into ours holding an open umbrella as she breaks through the line of clouds, feet turned out, magnificent but totally unexplained. In fact, as she says to her own boss by way of reprimand, 'I never explain anything.'

I do wonder whether, once we've reached adulthood, we sometimes forget we still need good role models. It felt so natural as a child to have people both real and fictional to look up to and take inspiration from. Maybe I need someone like that now. I can't do it all on my own. There are some good ones around – following the example of Michelle Obama isn't going to do you any harm. But she's a bit too polite to really drag me back to my best self. You know what I mean – she's a bit too respectful and encouraging. And busy. I feel I could tell Michelle Obama anything, for sure, but then she'd just pat me on the arm and say, 'I think you know what you need to do' and be whisked away to her next appointment. Or perhaps Gwyneth Paltrow might provide some guidance, though I am still one jade egg down on a full set and I daren't keep looking . . .

One of the greatest compliments of my life came from my husband only a couple of years ago. He had been to the supermarket and taken our young son with him for the ride, meaning that, for an hour or so, I was alone. It had been a particularly busy time for both of us and, to be perfectly frank, some basic standards had slipped. So I took the opportunity to fly around the house, tidying up. I opened windows to let fresh air in. I wiped the surfaces. I even did a bit of light dusting. It wasn't a huge effort on my part, or terribly thorough, but it made me feel better and it made enough of a superficial difference for my husband to exclaim, upon walking in with two heavy shopping bags, 'Oh, it's like Mary Poppins has been!'

Well, I glowed, I'm not going to lie. Two little Poppins-esque pink of spots of pleasure appeared on my cheeks. I spent the rest of the day floating around feeling like a paragon of virtue. I was in control of my home, my life and myself – if not my son, who was already busy undoing my good work by cutting up an old magazine and pouring glitter all over it. But the point is, I felt good. I felt the way I used to as a kid when I tidied my bedroom and sat down to survey the order before me. I felt calm. I felt happy. Of course, disorder would return, but for this moment at least, all was well. I really felt like Mary Poppins.

Now, here in 2020, I find myself at a bit of a crossroads and I do think I need some help to recapture this feeling. Fast-forward 30 years from my 10-year-old self sitting smugly in my newly immaculate bedroom (always a short-lived state . . . ) and I have to admit, as I look about me now, things have again gone a little . . . awry. My underwear drawer is a mess of tangled old bikini tops I will never wear again, pre-pregnancy knickers and single socks. And I still sometimes push dirty laundry into a pile in the corner of the room, carefully laying a blanket over it so I can pretend it's not there. I have taken to cutting my own hair because I'm too lazy to go to the hairdressers. It looks fine from the front but I have occasionally caught sight of the back of my head in a lift mirror and immediately put my hood up. It's not that there is some serious deep-seated problem or trauma that requires professional help, and I am thankful for that to be sure. It's more just a sort of general slackening. I need tightening up a little. I need a lifestyle mechanic.

A couple of years ago, for example, I turned up to film a TV show with my dog, because we were making a show about walking. I made so little effort with my on-screen appearance that my dog ended up looking better than me. I didn't even brush my hair. When I saw the programme, I winced at any shot of me from behind because I was mass of un-ironed shirt and haystack split-ends. I hadn't brought any make-up with me and, given that I was going to be out in the sun all day, you'd think I would have brought some sun-cream, but no. You can clearly see that I am lobster-pink and sore by the last scene – I yelped when I saw it. I was a disgrace. I was embarrassed. I mean, it was also hilarious and god knows I've looked worse on TV many times, but the point is that was by design. This was by negligence.

And it's not just on a professional level, it's self-care too. I still eat too much rubbish; a McDonald's cheeseburger is not a 'snack', I try to tell myself, tiny though it undoubtedly is. Despite reading an article at least every 48 hours on the benefits of avocado, chilli, turmeric, live yoghurt, kimchi, sauerkraut, whole grains, miso and charcoal smoothies, I will still eat a croissant at any time of day if it is available to me. I like a Pot Noodle for lunch more often than is dignified. Crisps are a particular weakness. I drink every day apart from when I have my annual bout of norovirus (which I now consider a sort of de facto detox, as I lack the discipline to undertake one of my own free will). 'Enough is as good as a feast,' says Mary Poppins brightly to the Banks children. Can it ever be so?

Next on this list of my current flaws and weaknesses (good to have a good clear-out of one's character every now again, as well as your bedroom, I think): I don't open my post in a timely fashion because, like a student, I am still scared of it. I look at my finances sideways because I know I won't like what I see. Banks terrify me. And yet, though it is all unopened, I hoard post because I am too scared to throw it away – why? I'm not entirely sure, but it may stem from the time when I was twenty and I was threatened with legal action over an outstanding phone bill of £13.23, simply because I didn't want to look.

My final admission is that I can't pretend to be an exemplary parent. Not enough guided play, too much plastic-based crap that comes with children's magazines only to be used once then broken or trodden on and pushed under the sofa. Where are the plain wooden blocks with which to build an imagination? Where are the informative books with subtle watercolour illustrations of woodland scenes? Where did I put my phone again? NO! Get off the phone, this is not how it should be . . . I want to be better than this. I'd intended to be better than this.

I think I need to revisit some of my ambitions to be a more organised and effective sort of person. I need to pull myself together. My life has gone from Mary Poppins to Eddie Monsoon. There's much to be thankful for, but reader, I do not feel I am living my 'best life' at all. And not because of any massive external problem, but more . . . more . . . because I *can't be bothered*. That looks awful written down but I think it's true. I'm not living my best life because I've become too lazy. I need a kick up the bum, a stern look, a firm word. Firm, but kind, perhaps . . .

I can see that, at the age of 41, it is time to put some new habits in place. I sometimes feel that I made it this far on coffee, crisps, alcohol and sheer bloody-mindedness. But these days a hangover lasts three days and comes with a side order of existential despair. I find I can easily fall asleep almost anywhere at around 4.30pm every day. I have started making a noise when I kneel down and then another, slightly louder noise when I get up again. If I don't change something, it's not going to get better on its own.

I want to re-establish my boundaries, feel more in control and less like I am firefighting all the time. I want to remind myself to say no to things occasionally and to make time for holidays, for fun. I want to employ the Poppins Doctrine to make my life better, calmer and more productive.

I used to be terribly resourceful. I love DIY, for example, and I feel confident I could make basic furniture if required. In fact, one of the few things I learned from Guides before I was politely ejected was how to lash sticks together to make things. Never mind that the first thing we were made to construct when arriving in a field for Guide Camp was a washing-up stand, as if this was a basic tool for survival, the principles remain the same. It didn't seem strictly fair – it was obvious to anyone with a sense of smell that the scent of smoke rising from the nearby Scout Camp meant the boys were already setting fire to things. Nevertheless, these were valuable lessons. And I learned them. Well, some of them.

Brownie Camp was mainly dominated by chores. We would arrive in some remote hut and were divided into four groups before we had even got off the coach. It was a weekend of chores on rotation – cooking, washing up, tidying the hut, clearing up the garden – and almost nothing else save the occasional game of rounders. How I longed for that elusive 'element of fun'. Sugar was strictly rationed, of course.

I'm not entirely ungrateful. For example, because of Brownies, I was able to sew a button onto Les Dennis's shorts during a reality

TV show we did together. I was the only member of the group who knew how to do it. Someone even called me Mary Poppins. Can you imagine how hard it was not too look tearful with pride? I felt some of my feminist credentials, such as they are, slipping slightly – is it OK to feel proud of sewing on a man's button and still maintain the required level of outrage at historic inequality over domestic chores? The comedian and writer Deborah Frances-White's smash-hit podcast 'The Guilty Feminist' requires guests to say, 'I am a feminist, but . . . ' and then give an example of something that undermines their claim. Well, I've got mine now: 'I'm a feminist, but I was secretly bursting with pride when I sewed a button on Les Dennis's shorts.'

It's not just my bad habits I've realised I want to address. I'd also like to reconnect with some of my old sense of power, before it got battered, but the task feels daunting. I think there are plenty of us feeling a bit tired and rundown generally. It's been a tough few years, for me anyway. Whatever your political views, there is no doubt that the waters are choppy. Nothing feels certain. Things that would have sounded crazy at the start of the decade are just rolling by now. 'Police Arrest Man for Buying Easter Eggs' was a headline I saw this morning, in response to the lockdown measures imposed by the UK government during the Covid-19 crisis. I barely batted an eyelid. I feel a pervasive sense of general exhaustion and powerlessness, and I'm fairly sure it's not just me.

For women in particular, it's been a bruising time. The #MeToo movement has achieved so much since it was started in 2006 by Tarana Burke, but at times the seemingly constant revelations of sexual harassment and systematic abuses of power have felt immensely draining.

So many have said that from 2016 onwards, they feel the world has thrown blow after blow, and we are all punch-drunk, cowering a little and waiting for the next one to land. Reports of anxiety in people of all age groups are through the roof. Financial insecurity is a growing problem with many working several jobs on zero hours contracts just to get by, and thousands are taking on debt to cover the gaps. I am not immune to any of this – my industry is as insecure as anything and I have had some bad years in my career of twenty years. I know how tired it makes you. But there must be a way to throw some of it off and travel a little lighter.

Sometimes it's good to withdraw for a short while, and find some quiet, to gather the energy for a new push. This time of staying at home, isolating and reflecting, even if it is enforced, feels like a good moment to have a clear-out, and I have seen so many tweets and articles saying the same. Here is a moment to take stock and get rid of anything that doesn't feel helpful. Perhaps we can emerge better. Sometimes life hands us a time-out, not always under happy circumstances of course, but if we try it can be possible to use these periods to reflect and re-evaluate what matters, how we want to live in a big sense and also how satisfied we are by the way we handle our experience of the every day.

Even if I can't reduce my actual furniture down to whatever can fit in a carpetbag, I can certainly have a look at slimming down and off-loading some mental and emotional baggage. The world has stopped for a moment and instead of fighting it or becoming depressed and even more slob-like, instead of giving in to the temptation of simply changing from last night's pyjamas into tonight's pyjamas at around 9pm each day, I'd like to get a bit Mary Poppins on it all and take the opportunity to do some sorting out, to finally put some new, better habits in place, rather than allowing things to slide completely out of control. I'd like to borrow some of the Poppins fortitude and her stoic, practical approach to life's problems. I think she may be the heroine, the role model I need right now. It doesn't have to be hard. Just follow her example. As she would say herself, 'Why complicate things that are really quite simple?'

I want that invincible feeling back that I used to get as a child right after I watched *Mary Poppins*. I want to feel I can tackle these issues that prevent me from moving through life in a happier and more streamlined way. Because I have a pile of post to open, some dirty laundry to sort out, I'm still in my pyjamas and I can't face another moment of playing *Paw Patrol* with my youngest child. So I am going to watch the film again. I am going to sit down on this Tuesday afternoon and watch it – it seems the best way to begin. Perhaps I should be working on my novel or sitting on the exercise bike I bought six months ago and have ignored ever since (it still only has one pedal as I gave up assembling it) or making a batch of fig-based vegan energy balls, but I can feel Mary Poppins calling to me. Best not to ignore her.

# Chapter 2

# A Spoonful Of Sugar

So, here I am, about to watch *Mary Poppins* again for the first time in many years, in search of some life-guidance, a dose of her confidence and perhaps a reminder of a simpler time when I thought I knew what being an adult entailed and I was sure I would be good at it. I wonder what details I have remembered perfectly and what I have forgotten and what I will notice now with grown-up eyes that I didn't then. Will it have the same impact now on this somewhat world weary woman, this mother of two, this 'battle-hardened feminist' (ha ha), this wife, this lover of just 'one more biscuit and then that's definitely enough', as it did when I was young and innocent, and easily impressed by a singing robin and a dancing penguin or two?

I am going to effectively live-blog Mary Poppins for you. Are you ready? As Bert would say, 'Here we go . . . ' Or perhaps rather, 'Eyarr weay geeeoww!'

Well, the first and most obvious change is that I am scrolling through the menu of my digital streaming service rather than loading a slightly cracked VHS tape into a somewhat reluctant machine. Once, when I was travelling around rural Pakistan, I came upon a sheep and goat trading market, that also incongruously had a few stalls selling second-hand electronic equipment. I observed a shepherd who was interested in a VCR machine open the tape flap and peer inside, just as he had moments before with a sheep to check the quality of its teeth. And I felt at the time it made sense, because I too always had the sense that our video machine would bite my fingers off if I didn't let go of the tape immediately.

But anyway, the point is, times have changed. As has the quality of my viewing experience. The telly is bigger and louder for a start. I press play. It begins.

Bloody hell, I had forgotten that old films put the FULL CREDITS at the top of the film. With a full orchestral arrangement of the whole score playing underneath it. Now, as someone who works in the film industry, I admire this because it means when people watched in the cinema they had no choice but to see the name of every single person who worked on it (and I do mean EVERY SINGLE PERSON, including the assistant to the conductor, who I can tell you is called James MacDonald), which is at odds with how all the efforts of very important departments and people are ignored these days. The only names you will see at the start of films now are the stars, the producer and the director, and maybe the writer if they're lucky and/or have a very good agent.

But look, I'm not a saint. And I'm going to do what every normal person does: after about three minutes of enjoying the incredibly beautiful panoramic paintings of the London skyline at smoky dusk, I am going to fast-forward through them to the start of the actual film (pausing to check out our Mary sitting on a cloud high above, powdering her nose). I imagine the decline of this practice of putting the credits at the beginning of a film coincides almost exactly with the invention of a fast-forward function on the first home video devices. So now they are always tucked at the end.

Ah! It's Dick Van Dyke as Bert, bouncing around with his one-man-band kit, improvising little rhymes for a happy gang of well-to-do Edwardians, none of whom seem keen to throw coins in his cap. But now, what's this? Suddenly there's a change in the direction in the wind and this is the first tingle of excitement. Who doesn't love the idea that magical things can happen when the wind changes? And we know this Bert is in on something, that he's connected to or at least aware of the magic (would it be too much to mention again my long-standing crush on Bert, accent notwithstanding?) . . . Now he is staring at us directly from down the camera with his madly blue eyes and artfully grimy face. He's talking to us. He's suggesting we want to go to number 17 Cherry Tree Lane. He knows the way . . . off we go.

Here is a street full of wedding-cake houses and cherry trees frothed with blossom. With Bert as our guide, we pass Admiral Boom, stoking his cannon, ready to announce the time with a series of explosions. The prologue over, the sense of eccentricity and wonder established, we go inside the Banks household. The house is in chaos and the staff are in full domestic row mode; Katie Nanna is resigning – she can't handle the children a moment longer. There's the sound of singing outside and a ripple of fear runs through the servants. Mrs Banks is coming back from her meeting. The children are missing.

But forget all that, because – and this is striking me now, as never before – the first real musical number of this film is about . . . THE

SUFFRAGETTES! The first scene at Cherry Tree Lane is women singing about equal rights and it sets us up for one of the themes of *Mary Poppins* – women bringing chaos to the accepted order of things. And those lyrics to 'Sister Suffragette' are just superb: 'Though we adore men individually, we agree that as a group they're rather stupid.' The whole scene is magnificent, fun, cheeky, satirical – it's women having a wonderful time together. As a child, you soak it all up without really knowing that there's anything subversive about it, which is as it should be. As an adult, you have to stand back and admire it.

Meanwhile, George Banks is strolling home, blissfully unaware that his home and castle is in disorder. God is in his heaven and all is right with the world. He's happy and certain of everything. The Admiral asks how life is in the world of finance – 'Never better – the pound is envy of the world.' But we know he's about to step into madness. There is a warning in the Admiral's observation: 'The wind's changing – don't like the look of it. You're steering into a nasty bit of weather.' But ever-confident Banks ignores it. Even as he sings the self-congratulatory 'The Life I Lead' his wife is trying to tell him there is a problem. He ignores her, he doesn't want to hear it – 'King Edward's on the throne and it's the age of men!' Now we know this film is going to be about women throwing all the nicely arranged furniture in the air to see where it lands. It's a lovely juxtaposition with 'Sister Suffragette'. Mr Banks may still believe in the 'Age of Men' but Mrs Banks can feel the sand shifting under their feet. Men think they are in charge, but the reality is very different.

The children, Jane and Michael, are missing, but not for long. Here they are – the friendly local bobby has brought them back.

Domestic order is temporarily restored. Mr Banks will wrest back control and all will be well. He will get a new nanny. But the children have other ideas and appear with their own advertisement to put in *The Times*.

Oh, I do love these kids, Michael with his soft little smile, and Jane sounding like a combination of Mary Berry and Kirstie Allsopp. They have a list of demands, regarding taking them on outings and bringing sweets. I still don't really know what barley water smells like but they are sure the new nanny must not give off a whiff of it. They have a kind of impertinent cuteness that never tips into sugary. With the ad rejected by Dad, it's ripped up and thrown into the fireplace. They are crushed and sent back to the nursery.

Mr Banks calls *The Times* to place his advertisement. He grabs at his wall-mounted phone with no dial and barks, 'Give me *The Times* please – no, I do NOT know the number!'

'Oh George, you're always so forceful,' Mrs Banks whispers huskily.

One of the things I love about this is how obviously utterly minxy Mrs Banks is. It sort of makes you like Mr Banks more – how bad can he be, if this is his wife?

But behind him the torn-up pieces of the children's advertisement are starting to mingle in an updraft in the fireplace, they are lifting ever so slightly and now they're disappearing up the chimney in a column of air.

In the next scene it is the next morning and a long line of potential nanny-rivals has assembled outside the Banks' front door. But the wind is getting up and weather vane is swinging. The nannies are being blown away and now, what's this? Why, it's Mary Poppins floating down over London while Jane and Michael watch out of their nursery window, mouths agape. 'Perhaps she's a witch,' says Michael – perhaps indeed. She lands, feet perfectly turned out, snaps her umbrella shut and walks towards number 17.

I'm going to have to pause it for a minute. I cannot keep up. We are about twenty minutes in and there's been enough action for about an entire modern children's film. Snap, snap, snap – this story doesn't sit still for a minute. No wonder I loved it as a kid – it just keeps pulling you on. And there's so much to look and wonder at. So much bloody bang for your buck. No wonder it is often referred to as 'Walt Disney's crowning achievement'. No wonder the profits from *Mary Poppins* alone went to fund the construction of Disney World. How could anyone not fall in love with this?

Anyway, settle down, settle down, she's here. She walks into the Banks' house like a duchess. It's exciting, and it was exciting too as a child, to see how few shits she gives. Julie Andrews really is so very good at this. I think there is some notion that she is all goody-two-shoes, bright eyes and white teeth and a voice like a bell on a clear Alpine day, but there's so much more to her than that. She's pure tight sass and she doesn't even have to wiggle.

To Mr Banks' surprise, he finds she is interviewing him to see if *she* wants to be nanny to his children. After she informs him that she 'never provides references' (god, I have wished to be able to say that a few times in my life), he patronises her back but retribution comes fast – she has in her hands the advert the children wrote that he tore up and put in the fireplace. She has pieced it together. She is issuing her demands. He is losing his mind. She stares at him, and here's one of my favourite lines. She asks, 'I beg your pardon, are you ill?' I have used this line before on people who I think are acting rudely and I have to say it works rather well.

Despite her reservations about Mr Banks, she accepts the position, walks out, sits on the bannister and slides up it gracefully to meet the children, whose eyes are on stalks. And George Banks is starting to feel that something is afoot . . . his grip is loosening. The man has lost a little bit of control over his castle but, as he fills his pipe, he cannot yet conceive of what is to come.

To the nursery. Mary Poppins has her carpet bag out. I always loved this bag – unsurprisingly really considering I am someone whose own husband refers to her handbag as 'the TARDIS'. To carry all these things around like this – a standard lamp, a large gilt mirror, a hat-stand, an aspidistra in a brass pot – is marvellous. To be so self-sufficient and to be able to instantly turn a room that is drab and faceless into a cosy space with luxurious touches to me is a skill indeed.

But what does it mean? Is she homeless? Or between places? Is this all that she owns in the world? If so, congratulations, because she has Marie Kondo'd the shit out of her life. As someone who has recently had to admit to a hoarding instinct I'm jealous. Our last house move required seven skips to get rid of all the stuff I had accumulated. For the love of god, I can't think where we were keeping it in the house. We had a whole other house worth of stuff shoved into bags and cupboards, most of it old and broken and useless to anyone. So, to carry all your stuff around in one bag is impressive, even if the bag is essentially bottomless. These are questions that will never be answered though.

Jane and Michael's nursery isn't awful by any stretch of the imagi-nation, but Mary's room is a bit dreary. She can perk it up with a few well-chosen items. If you move around a lot, you have to adapt – that's what she's showing us. And also, perhaps, that it's a good idea to carry with you the things you require, and not expect them to suddenly materialise whenever you need them . . .

During my twenties, I lived in many different places and some were grim. I once rented a room in a flat in London with a window that was fewer than six inches from the wall of the next house, so I had no natural light at all. I couldn't afford a bed frame so I had a mattress on the floor and, during my time there, my asthma mysteriously worsened. About a month after I moved out, I heard that the owners had been forced to demolish all the internal walls as the flat was mouldy from floor to ceiling. You could have made a serviceable risotto with the mushrooms growing under the carpet. And yet for my six-month tenancy, I put in a pot plant, a cheap rug from Home Bargains and a nice big David Hockney poster of a swimming pool – my own equivalent of the standard lamp, mirror, hat-stand and aspidistra I suppose – and I felt much better . . . once I had taken my inhaler.

This is perhaps the first important lesson Mary Poppins teaches us – with a few little bits and pieces you can make anywhere all right for a bit. And a lick of paint. I have redecorated every house I've ever lived in. In fact, one house I redecorated from top to bottom three times over the course of six years. And when I say 'I', I don't mean like when the Queen says, 'It was cold so I lit a fire in here,' I mean, I actually painted the walls myself. And I enjoyed every minute. It's very reassuring to know you can control and change your environment yourself with a bucket of paint and the will to stick it on the walls . For this reason, I have almost bankrupted myself in Homebase on several occasions. I feel certain I got this from Mary Poppins.

Now then, let's get a good look at her because she's taken off her coat. For a woman who appears to travel by cloud, she's remarkably well put together. It's pretty bold to only really start to introduce the title character of the film nearly half an hour in. But she's worth waiting for, right? First of all, she is so pleasingly neat. Every item of clothing fits her perfectly – has she made it all herself? Does she have a seamstress? I could only wish to look this well put together. These days I congratulate myself if I brush my hair and put on a pair of trousers with a button and a zip. Tights are saved for only the most special of occasions as, although I wish I could be one of those women who sits lightly on the side of the bed, rolls a pair of tights down to the toe and then daintily places her foot in them and slides the rest up her leg like a condom on a porn star, realistically they take me twenty minutes of full body contortion to put on. But Poppins is everything I wish I could be. Perfectly crisp pie-crust collar. A tiny velvet bow at her throat, tied with fierce and uncompromising symmetry. Puff-shouldered jacket, a sweeping, long, A-line skirt with a hem straighter than Jack Nicholson. And then those boots! Now, I have a shoe fetish. It's not a secret; I have discussed it openly on BBC Radio 4. And those hobnailed boots just spell 'together' to me.

So, not a hair out of place. Make-up perfectly set – natural, rosy-cheeked. We can drink her in as she admires her own reflection in the mirror, which comes to life and admires her back. Just marvel at the level of confidence here. What would it take to break her? Is there a chink in this armour at all? No time to find out, because now here is a moment to really savour: the tape measure, which has given me the title of this very book. For as we all know very well, when Mary Poppins gets her tricksy tape-measure out, we find that she measures 'practically perfect in every way'. Can you imagine telling a couple of kids you had just met and had already seen off a dozen hard-wearing nannies that you are 'practically perfect in every way' and getting away with it? Could I ever achieve this heady level of self-confidence in my own life?

The nursery is a mess and Mary Poppins will not tolerate a mess. But tidying doesn't have to be boring – 'Find the fun,' Mary tells us, clicking her fingers. And that finger snap! All I wanted to do when I was ten was to be able to snap my fingers with that level of conviction and volume. Like little Michael, I tried and tried. I got a good one about 5 per cent of the time, but when it happened – what a joy! Even if my bedroom never got any tidier. This was one of my favourite scenes as a child. What small person has not watched this sequence agog, as the messy nursery clears itself up? 'A Spoonful of Sugar' is bouncing around and we hear *that* singing voice for the first time – so perfect and so clear. And as this was Julie Andrews' first Hollywood film role, this would have been the first time most of the film's cinema audiences had heard it, too.

An outing now and down the bannisters they go, sliding smoothly as Poppins checks her hair. I remember going into some grand old house – a National Trust property perhaps on a Sunday outing – and seeing a grand staircase and thinking, 'That's a Mary Poppins ban-nister,' which meant 'good for sliding'. I so desperately wanted to give it a go but I could sense that would not have gone down well. They're heading for the park and here's Bert again, now a pavement chalk artist. 'I does what I likes, and I likes what I do,' he sings.

And then Mary steps into the picture, literally, creating a perfect silhouette. They are pleased to see each other, it's all a bit flirty. 'You'll go to places you've never dreamed of,' he says – what HAS been going on with Bert and Mary? And here's the first of what I am calling the 'Mary Poppins Gaslighting Events', where she simply refuses to acknowledge or confirm something that has been directly witnessed by others, often leaving them visibly questioning their own sanity. 'I'm sure I haven't the faintest idea what you're talking about,' she responds to Bert and that shuts him up. I always liked this about her – 'deny, deny, deny'. Just keep crisply saying, 'I don't know what you're talking about' while looking stern, and eventually they'll drop it. It is the first of many.

We're jumping into the pavement scene of a beautiful day out in the country and here's some proper hallucinatory magic. Our four characters – now in fun new outfits – are surrounded by bright colours and gorgeous animation. This is really Disney off the leash – cute bunnies, dancing waiter penguins, a bouquet of flowers that turns into hundreds of butterflies, friendly turtles who will carry you across a babbling stream on their backs – on and on, just drink it in.

Bert and Mary are having a little sexy flirt (though not too sexy, as it was banned by both P L Travers and Julie Andrews, and I think on balance they were right). She does refer to him in the song that follows – 'Jolly Holiday' – as a gentleman she feels safe with. 'You'd never think of pressing your advantage.' There is something a bit frisky about this song, though of course nothing happens. Instead, as author Jenny Colgan points out on Twitter, it is a 'nine-minute opus about how Bert is never, ever getting his end away'. I now see the truth of this and notice Mary's steely-firm rejection of any sort of funny business.

The horse-race begins and is won by Mary on one of the horses that has left the carousel, then it's 'Supercalifragilisticexpialidocious' and then we're back in London, in the rain. Watching this as an adult, it strikes me how gorgeous this idea is – that the rain will come and wash away the dream, ready for a new picture to be drawn. For me now, the ravishing painting of the London backdrops probably trumps the animation in terms of sheer breathtaking skill, but I have a feeling ten-year-old me would not agree.

Now we're back in the nursery, a fire burning in the grate, clean bedclothes, and medicine. And then, the moment of ultimate mystery – Michael asks how long Mary Poppins will be around. And she replies, 'I shall stay until the wind changes.' Why? Does the wind control you, Mary Poppins? Or do you make the wind? Or are you acting in co-operation with the wind? We will never know.

The agony and ecstasy of this leads us into Mary Poppins Gaslighting Event Number Two. As the children share reminiscences of the day, Poppins is indignant. She flat out denies it: 'A respectable person like me in a horse race? How dare you suggest such a thing. Now, not another word or I shall have to summon a policeman.' A line so camp it makes me spontaneously laugh out loud. This is followed by the lullaby, 'Stay Awake' – the safety of this after the danger of the day. The children are sung to sleep by Julie Andrews in her starched house-coat, warm and snug. She is a perfect nanny, again, and nothing is amiss.

Another day. Another explosion from Admiral Boom. 'Put in a double charge of powder – shake things up a bit, what?' he declares, in a nice little nod to the metaphorical thread that runs through the whole film – it's *all* about shaking things up, I see that now.

'We're all going to Downing Street to throw things at the prime minister!' shouts minxy Mrs Banks as she struts out of the house without a backward glance. Everyone is happy this morning except for Mr Banks. The effect of Mary Poppins' presence has buoyed the women but irritated the man of the house. 'I just can't understand why everyone's so confoundedly cheerful.' He has a headache. Something's shifted. There's a new and powerful female energy here and it's rippling outwards.

On with the day's outing and of course it's hijacked by talking dog Andrew (excellent name) who runs up to pass on an urgent message to Mary Poppins. If you never really got the whole Andrew thing, he is a bigger feature in the original books where he lives with an old lady neighbour to the Banks family, who spoils him rotten and won't let him play with his doggie friends for fear that he will become corrupted. But anyway, who doesn't love a talking dog?

Andrew takes us to Uncle Albert's. This scene, where the children and Bert and eventually Mary join Uncle Albert, who seems to have become weightless with laughter, for a tea party on the ceiling fascinates me – it doesn't add anything at all to the story, it's just a sketch, sort of dumped in the middle. It's fun though, and this feeling of there being a secret underworld in London of magical people all connected to Mary Poppins always gave me a lovely little shiver. It still does now.

Now we're back at Cherry Tree Lane and Jane and Michael have been waiting to tell their father the jokes they heard. But, unsurprisingly, they do not go down well. I suppose this is the purpose of the Uncle Albert scene in a way – Mr Banks' alarm and incomprehension at these crazy stories his children are telling him focuses his disquiet around Mary Poppins and leads to . . . the attempted sacking! Mr Banks is going to try to sack Mary Poppins.

I sit at her feet and MARVEL at the way she turns this whole thing to her advantage. The sheer brass balls on her. She's so plausible. By the end of the conversation she's bamboozled him into keeping her on and taking his children on a trip to the bank the next day. It is still really exciting to watch her manipulate him like this without so much as breaking a sweat – surely this is Gaslighting Event Number Three? She is about to be fired, yet by the end of the encounter she has kept her job and also wangled herself an extra day off. And I laugh out loud as she returns to the nursery to find Jane and Michael clamouring to comfort her after her dismissal, only to be rebuked with, 'Sacked? Certainly not, I am never sacked.' Beautiful.

And here's a contender for the most perfect song in *Mary Poppins*, and one of the greatest in cinema history (it was certainly Walt Disney's personal favourite): 'Feed the Birds'. Oh god, I'm welling up already. It's immediately obvious to me as an adult that this is the real beating heart of the film, its reason for being, for it has a triple meaning. There's the literal meaning of feeding the birds, of course, but also an exhortation to parents to spare a little attention and tenderness for their own 'little birds' who need feeding with love. And finally, a subversive lesson in inequality, poverty and social responsibility, in direct contrast to the previous song, sung by George Banks, 'A British Bank'. This is all delivered to a pair of impressionable children on the eve of a visit to their father's work, which happens to be a temple to capitalism. It's hard to believe Poppins doesn't know exactly what she's doing here . . . Poppins is a political agitator. Who knew?

The next morning, the children leave with their father for a visit to the bank. As they walk to work, Mr Banks explains that they must be on best behaviour. All is going well and then they see the Bird Woman, just as Mary Poppins described. Like some kind of Derren Brown, she has planted a seed deep in the sleeping children's minds, she has hypnotised them with her lilting voice and now we are going to see the consequences play out. It's a delicious little bit of scripting – the writers must have been hugging themselves.

We arrive at the stuffy bank, and here we have Dick Van Dyke's performance as the old man of the place (he was so desperate to play this role he begged Disney to allow it . . . come on, admit how old you were when you realised?). He wants Michael's tuppence but Michael won't give it to him. In 'Fidelity Fiduciary Bank' they sing him a song about all the things his money will buy if it is invested with them, such as 'railways in Africa', 'plantations of ripening tea'. The confusion on Michael's face is an absolute picture. All he can see is a bunch of men who want to get their crepey hands on his tuppence. I can sympathise. He wants to spend it with the bird lady. He's firm on this. He runs out of the building shouting, which initiates a run on the bank, causing total chaos and ultimately costing his father his job, his hat and his dignity. And Mary Poppins made this happen. Where is she now? What's she doing?

Jane and Michael have escaped and now they are lost in the back-streets of London amid mad old ladies and dogs barking. Though *Oliver!* was made in 1968, four years after *Mary Poppins*, and set a little earlier too, somehow I always think of it here – how close the London of Oliver Twist is to the London of Jane and Michael. It feels like, any moment, they could stumble into Fagin's den, and never be seen again. All these versions of the city, all these realities, exist side by side. They still do.

And then a sooty-faced figure is grabbing at Jane. It's lovely Bert; today he's a chimney sweep with some wisdom about being a man alone in the world, about how hard it is to be a father – 'When something terrible happens, who does he talk to? No one, that's who.' His words make a visible impression on the children and, as an adult, I realise how pivotal this is both to the plot and the emotional resonance of the film. Bert takes them home to find Mrs Banks about to go out to another one of her meetings. And, oh god, this is hilarious – I'd forgotten this – instead of gathering them in and making sure they are unharmed after their frightening experience alone in London, she asks the maid to look after them, who refuses. She remembers it's Mary Poppins' day off and just asks Bert to look after them instead – a man who is a stranger to her at this point. Brilliant. She is a total law unto herself, this woman.

Heading into 'Chim Chim Cher-ee' and we're on the rooftops – this is the greatest all-round sequence in the film, for my money – great song, great dancing and ravishing backdrops such as the gleaming white dome of St Paul's, appearing through the smoky chimney stacks. And here's a staircase made of soot that carries them up high into the sunset sky with a view across all of London. 'There's a whole world at your feet and who gets to see it but the stars, the birds and chimney sweeps,' says Bert, as he gazes out at the astounding vista. What a line – a chimney sweep is richer than a banker because he's free.

Here come Bert's mates, a bit of mad 'Step in Time' dancing, includ-ing possibly the earliest example of parkour on film, and Poppins in a foreshadowing moment of toe-dancing Kate Winslet in *Titanic*, besting the lot of them – all ended prematurely by Admiral Boom going a bit nuts with his cannon and scaring them off.

Back in the Banks' living room, there's proper trouble. Chimney sweeps are everywhere, dancing with Mrs Banks, singing 'Votes for Women' (swoon). Mr Banks arrives home from the worst day of his life to find his house full of filthy men and sweating women. Even Mary Poppins seems to know she's gone too far this time but she rallies and brazens it out: 'I never explain anything,' she says firmly with a glare, and marches up the stairs.

As a result of the earlier chaos at the bank, George is summoned back to the office, at '9pm precisely'. I always thought this seemed very late for a meeting, but what did I know of the world of adults and banking? Perhaps professional people always met this late.

'A man has dreams,' this sad, melancholy song begins and suddenly we are pulled into feeling sorry and frightened for pompous, deluded old Mr Banks. He thought he had everything figured out but now it's a mess – Mary Poppins arrived with 'chaos in her wake' (such a beautiful line). He blames her for everything. And now he and Bert are having a little heart-to-heart.

This is another scene I had forgotten – or that perhaps made less of an impression on me as a child than the excitement and bells and whistles of the other songs. Through sympathising with Mr Banks' position as a busy man, Bert subtly plants the seed of an idea in his head that working all the time isn't necessarily the path to happiness and there is another way – a progressive world, in which men pay attention to their children and their feelings. It's a beauty. Do Bert and Mary work in tandem all the time, I find myself wondering . . . ? Bert is suddenly singing 'A Spoonful of Sugar' whilst pretending to be largely ignorant of her methods. Is he manipulating George too? Dammit, more questions with no answers.

Either way, this is pivotal and Mr Banks seems to really take on board Bert's tactful message. Here are his cute kids in clean pyjamas with a tuppence to give him. They know he is in trouble. 'Will that make everything all right?' asks Jane, with heart-breaking naivety.

'Thank you,' he replies, with heart-breaking restraint. He knows it won't. He heads out into the rain-soaked London streets to meet his doom. He unknowingly passes Uncle Albert's house – they live side by side, muggles and magicians. Two worlds reaching for each other but not quite meeting unless Poppins is there. And we are far from the laughter of friends now. This adult world is bleak and forbidding.

And here it is represented in the central organs of the bank, with dark lighting and red velvet, intimidating and humourless. Banks gets his bollocking – curiously violent, isn't it? The punch through the hat, the cutting of the flower, the destruction of the umbrella. Is this really how bankers behave at work? It's possible. And he is sent packing, but not before he has made himself hysterical. 'Supercalifragilisticexpialidocious!' he bursts out, as the incidental music changes from something dirge-like to 'Feed the Birds'. Banks appears to be having a breakdown, but possibly the good kind. He tells a joke, presses the tuppence into the old man's hand and is gone, babbling nonsense. Dancing home in his demeaned delirium, he shouts about how wonderful Poppins is.

Ah, but the wind is changing, the weather vane is moving again. We know what that means. And sure enough, we're cutting to the nursery where Poppins is packing her bags and the children are crying. 'Mary Poppins, don't you love us?'

'And what would happen to me, may I ask, if I loved all the children I said goodbye to?' she replies. Wow. Not much sugar here. P L Travers was insistent that Poppins was never sentimental, and she wasn't joking.

And downstairs, in a nice echo of the first scene, we have the policeman calling about a missing Mr Banks. He's been gone for hours. And now he's back, singing all Mary Poppins' songs without a care in the world. He's been in the cellar. He's fixed the broken kite from scene one.

We're pulling it all together, all the strands. Mr Banks has his family back, his wife by his side, his happy children and a mended kite. And now perhaps one of the most bizarre conclusions I have ever seen in a film, where they happily skip out to join a huge party of people, including all Mr Banks' colleagues from the bank, who are apparently all also flying kites. Is this a thing? Was this a thing? I shall investigate. But never mind for now – Mrs Banks attaches her Votes for Women sash to the kite and up it goes – lovely – that message soaring away, high above a changing London. Banks gets his job back along with a promotion. Everyone is so very, very happy.

And we return to Mary Poppins, on the doorstep, being delivered home truths by her talking parrot umbrella. He wants to know if she's offended by their leaving without saying good bye. Her response – 'Practically perfect people never permit sentiment to muddle their thinking.' What a great thing to say.

'Don't stay away too long,' says Bert, looking up as she drifts over the London skyline. WHERE IS SHE GOING? We will never know. We will never know . . .

Oh, it's still a great film. It's quirky as ever, and jarring and mysterious. But also funny and reassuring. It doesn't age – it's both strange and familiar. And, like all great art, it endures and its message can adapt to changing times – you can find new themes that resonate within the context in which you are living. Because a family is universal, and what family doesn't need a little help from time to time?

I loved it all over again, of course. It felt like a tonic, somehow.

An antidote. Just as I did when I was ten, I suddenly find I want to clean the house and get a breath of fresh air. I want to create order. I feel that invincibility and power bubbling up again. *Mary Poppins* gives you a little lift and then a shove in the right direction. Spit-spot.

# Chapter 3

# Stay Awake

It turns out parenting is hard work. I think we can all agree on that now. No one is going to win the Pulitzer for pointing it out. It's boring, messy and often thankless, and it always has been. What it hasn't always been is a lonely pursuit for two, or even one person to undertake without much help – living in larger family groups was more commonplace, or closer communities would assume some collective responsibility for all the children in a small area, keeping an eye out while they played, herding lost ones back to the right house. But for some reason, the modern way is to try to do it all by ourselves, or at least to pretend we are, with the occasional bit of input from a grandparent, a friend or – sod it – an agency babysitter, when you realise in horror that you haven't been out alone with your other half for well over a year. It's become a private affair, rather than the effort of a 'village', so to speak.

It is now a badge of honour to be totally across your child's life, regardless of whether you are an internationally successful model or in charge of a global finance conglomerate (is there such a thing as a global finance conglomerate? I don't know; it sounds plausible. I expect Mr Banks would be happy to explain). In fact, it's not just parenting, it's everything. Life feels complicated and relentless. There's a lot to do all the time. Keeping myself going feels impossible some days, let alone nurturing the next generation.

The point is, we seem to feel this pressure to be doing it *all* ourselves now – and the basics are no longer enough. We must of course put food on the table, keep up with the bills and not die prematurely, but it doesn't stop there. Forget *having* it all – that is a distant, selfish dream. Now it's about *doing* it all – dropping your child off at school and picking them up, doing all the household chores and making home-cooked meals whilst holding down a full-time job and providing structured play at the weekends, enjoying a satisfying sex life with your partner, making sure you see your family and maintain friendships, doing some voluntary work, saving the environment, offering your spare room to a refugee, campaigning to save the NHS, understanding what an ISA is and having an edifying and absorbing hobby. And knitting now, apparently. We're all supposed to know how to knit. I don't know who is out there really doing it all, but meanwhile, I am attempting to give it my all, whilst simultaneously failing at everything, and falling apart in the process. Net result: zero.

Is doesn't feel like a surprise that many people are now reporting feeling 'burnt out'. It's not just millennials, it's everybody, from Boomers to Generation X-ers and on, down to newborn babies, probably, who now clamber out of the womb and can barely draw their first breath before being put on social media sites and pinged around the world for likes. It's pressure all the time these days, for parents, children, godparents, aunts, uncles, grandparents. We are required to perform and participate – and be seen to be doing so. The extra non-essential daily tasks stack up and in the end it feels easier to tweet about baking than to actually make a cake. Thinking about and planning how to present my life, my family, my spare time is now so tiring and time consuming that I end up doing nothing that I was intending to do. I feel the urge to simplify. I want to throw everything away, cut off all my hair and start again.

I mean, I won't, but I should at least examine why I'm feeling like this, and what I can do about it.

What I yearn for, in the first instance, what would really make a difference, is a very good tidy-up – straight from the Mary Poppins play book. Like almost everyone else I know, I want a clean, cool home where everything has its place. This fantasy is clutter-free, with a few well-chosen pieces to provide decorative points of interest. I imagine a kitchen with well-ordered cupboards full of labelled goods well within their best before date and definitely not a mound of free-range lentils at the back from a split bag that may be providing food for a mouse. The bathroom and loo are spotless, even under the seat. Bed linen is fresh. Dust-bunnies are sucked up with a handheld hoover before they can breed, and as for cobwebs – in the fantasy house you will never have to make a joke to your neighbour who pops round about 'still having the Hallowe'en decorations up' the following June. It is utterly pristine at all times.

I have been in houses like this before and I have noticed the one thing they all have in common is this: staff.

For most of us, the very idea of having staff is an expensive dream. Or maybe it feels a bit naff, or like cheating. Some think it is downright immoral these days, and fair enough. Even admitting to having a weekly cleaner can be a source of great tension sometimes. But all this 'No, no – I do it all myself. Domestic servitude of other women is not part of the feminist dream' is a relatively recent idea. There are many accounts of women who would have considered themselves to be middle or even working class in the immediate past who still had what they might have called a 'daily'.

I have been a cleaner myself, going to a nice lady's house twice a week after school to collect £15 cash for three hours cleaning – of which I managed about 90 minutes and then snuck out. My aversion to mopping was so great I would clean the kitchen floor with a whole kitchen roll, sheet by sheet, and then hold the mop head under the running tap to avoid detection. Unsurprisingly, she let me go. I was ultimately better suited to pub work.

But the fact is, I can't achieve my dream of the minimalist household, or at least not consistently. Maybe about once a month, for half an hour, my house is about 70 per cent as clean, tidy and ordered as I would like it to be. Then, shortly after, chaos creeps in and, before I know it, I can't find my keys again.

I admit that I am a bit lazy, there's no getting away from it. I could keep it tidier but somehow wine seems to make the mess go away on its own, at least until the morning. And I am known for my 'piles of things' and 'bowls of crap' as my sister refers to them. She says she knows it's only a matter of time when I move in somewhere new before the 'bowls of crap' (coins, hair clips, broken sunglasses, single pieces of Lego, batteries of indeterminate age and functionality) start to emerge and multiply. She is entirely correct. I am fighting a losing battle, and I am fighting it with myself.

It was observed by a film executive I knew that one of the main components of success for a romantic comedy is how nice the houses of the characters are. If your leading lady lives in a beautiful, spacious home with an expansive kitchen, a well-appointed den and an elegant bedroom, the film does better at the box office. I'm as embarrassed about this as you are, but we can't hide from the cold, economic truth that we like looking at nice tidy houses because, from a certain age onwards, that's what we all really want, more than smooth thighs or a husband.

But these houses are a lie, a fiction and a fantasy. They are not houses that anyone real lives in. They are something to aspire to – like Reese Witherspoon's shiny hair, or Rihanna's smooth skin – but impossible to achieve. Unless of course they are created, supported and maintained by an experienced team of professionals. Which brings me back to my main point – that we are trying to do too much by ourselves. If you do not and are not likely to have access to such professionals, these are the options: give up; lower your standards; delegate within the household to any available children; or pay someone to come and help. We have to bite the bullet and admit it's not possible to do it perfectly alone.

In fact, I do think one of the marvels of *Mary Poppins* is the idea you could live your life like Mrs Banks and have all this help and that it was fine, expected, even. The Banks family is middle class and they can afford it all on Mr Banks' salary. I'm middle class, and yet somehow finances will still not stretch to three full-time, live-in staff in a detached house in west London.

The point is that the Banks family live in a time when it was expected that middle-class families would have a fully staffed house. Which shows you how far the definition of 'middle class' has changed since 1910. It's now become somewhat taboo to have a full-time, live-in nanny and some even get all Judgy-McJudgy pants about having professional childcare at all. Which leads the rich and famous to lie about it and the rest of us to pretend we didn't want a night nurse anyway. But back in 1910, it would have been considered a pretty poor show (and an immense embarrassment for Mr Banks) for a woman like Mrs Banks to do the nitty-gritty of looking after her own children.

I know this now. But watching as a child, I drank it all in. The order, the precision, the sense of a team of people running a well-oiled machine, everybody with a role to play. It was so unlike anything I had seen before at the time. It's one of the only films I can think of watching repeatedly where the staff are so central. The story is all about what happens when Mum and Dad are busy elsewhere, which is always exciting for a child. But watching now as an adult, as a parent, all I can do is stare at the tidy living room, the dining table free of clutter, the staff walking around with piles of fresh linen and feather dusters. It's like a fantasy of a whole different order.

I suppose we all stumble through the first couple of years of our children's lives and then start to wonder whether if we cut back on all the bills and didn't really eat anything except dried noodles and milk, we could afford a full-time, live-in nanny – other people's judgement be damned. Forget the maid and the cook, we can manage without them and, apart from anything else, I have a partner who does way more than his share on the domestic front. But seriously, can you imagine life with a full-time, live-in nanny? My god, it would be like not having kids at all. I'd have had loads of children with a full-time nanny around – I'd have just fired them out and then gone to the cinema every afternoon, popping my head round the door of the nursery on the way out to check they were alive and vaguely recognised me. I JOKE OF COURSE.

In reality, like most of us, I know I'd find having full-time, live-in staff supremely awkward, as well as unaffordable. I have experienced it briefly once or twice and it is a bit weird – like being in a hotel suite with someone from housekeeping who never, ever finishes or leaves. But the vision of the Banks home can still be an inspiration to me to sort it out myself. I am never going to live in a ridiculously high-ceilinged Edwardian home, replete with a polished bannister and festooned with crocheted doilies, but that doesn't mean I can't do what I can with what I've got. I'm sure this is what Mary Poppins would expect. And I managed it in that grotty flat in Clapham.

In some ways, I want to do it myself anyway. I think many of us share a secret love of bringing order to the home – achievable goals make you happy, I'm told, and there is nothing more 'achievable goals' than a pile of dirty washing up: you start with first plate and you keep going until it's all done. Unlike the pile of work assignments building in my inbox, which will never feel complete even when I have submitted them, you can't argue with a physical stack that moves from one side of the sink to the other – dirty to clean. When it's done, it's done. Truly, the secret to contentment.

Maybe deep down I want to do it myself because I want to be Mary Poppins rather than Mrs Banks. I want to be the one who sorts things out. I mean, I still want to go out for a cocktail every now and again, but I also want to be playing this role I loved as a child.

She is a seductive example to follow. She never tires, she never moans, she never eats crisps whilst hiding in a wardrobe so the children won't see them and want some. In fact, we can go further than Mary Poppins, and say that in one woman we have the perfect parenting template, because when it comes to childcare, Julie Andrews unites the only two models you will ever need: Mary Poppins, for your basic tidy your bedroom, undermine capitalism and start a run on the bank stuff; and Maria von Trapp in *The Sound of Music* for your climbing trees, singing in the mountains, shagging your employer and escaping from the Nazis sort of business. Between these two, I feel all eventualities are covered. And the best thing about it all is that, in both these films, Andrews is an exemplar of motherhood, without actually being anyone's biological mother. So we are all included, with our modern, messy, glorious blended families.

One of the Poppins superpowers is that she can turn on a dime, leaving her young charges unsettled and on the back foot, allowing her to keep control at all times. For example, during the iconic 'Spoonful of Sugar' scene, Poppins brings a chaotic solution to create a new order, tidying up the nursery with magic. Then, as things go a bit mad following an over-enthusiastic bout of finger-snapping by the children, she bellows the line, 'WHEN YOU'VE QUITE FINISHED!' And they stop. It's impressive and, what's more, I found out it works for us mere mortals too. I tried this very line last week in a direct impression of Mary Poppins on three naughty children in my care and it worked! Helpfully, they have no idea where it comes from because they are too young to have seen it yet.

The phrase 'firm but kind', as found on Jane and Michael's list of nanny requests, is something I have been thinking about a lot. It seems like a good parenting ambition. Poppins has a tone of voice, a purse of the lips, an angle of the eyebrow that seems to convey a natural authority. She never panics. She never shouts (well, just that once, but it is aimed at an errant, enchanted Jack-in-a-box, so does it really count?). And, most of all, best of all, she is not trying to be the children's friend.

I am not a fan of 'best friend parenting'. I think it's weird. I have such a deep aversion to it that I have to wonder where it came from and I am now ready to concede that it may have been formed by my early viewings of *Mary Poppins*. She would never dream of being 'friends' with the children. To be a friend, you have to be equal, and if I'm *legally in charge* of someone, we are not equal. If I know not to stick a fork into an electrical socket or that Play-Doh isn't edible and you don't, then I am the superior party. And the responsible party. I can be friend-ly. But we are not friends. Bottom line is: in an emergency, you do what I say.

Re-watching *Mary Poppins*, I realised with a bit of a surprise that to achieve a certain level of authority it helps to look the part. It's not enough to give a child a sharp glance because if you are a sartorial mess you have lost before you start. In my mind, I may be wearing that perfect pie-crust collar and a flawless housecoat, but it is clear to any five-year-old that I am still in my pyjamas at midday. This, I thought, may explain why, when I am giving it my full Poppins whilst picking scrambled egg off my nightie, the effect is somewhat lost. It must be confusing for a child, especially if they are immaculately dressed by 8am and asking, 'When is Mummy getting in the shower?' When I realised this, I resolved to do better.

There is a degree of self-respect that comes into play here and that is what Mary Poppins is so good at. She is clearly in charge of herself – everything about her demeanour, her appearance implies it – and so you feel confident in letting her take charge elsewhere. If you exhibit self-respect, even in the smallest ways, you can expect, or are entitled to, a higher level of respect from others. Or, at the very least, a five-year-old to whom you actually gave birth.

I will never forget visiting the home of a good friend who is a full-time mum to three children and being very, VERY aware of how well put together she was all the time I was there, which was five whole days. Now, I'm never going to go full-make-up, Gucci belt and heels because . . . because . . . just no. But I realised after that trip that I could and probably should do a lot better than my current 'work from home' uniform of stretchy trousers and yesterday's jumper, where bra = optional; hairbrush = lost weeks ago. It's fine from time to time, but I have to admit, it's now all the time. It's not impressive. I don't feel good about it. I don't think Mary Poppins would approve. She would see a slob and I would struggle to disagree. I'm not trying to be judgemental here – if it works for you, then fine. But I'm not sure it does work for me. I think I have just fallen into bad habits. I am going to give it go. I will leave you here, with hold music.

Some weeks later . . .

So, in this spirit of giving my life a Spring Poppins, and setting a better example for my children, I have now started to shower before 8.30am, put proper clothes on (including a proper bra) every day, brush my hair and even apply a very small amount of make-up (mascara – I'm not one for contouring, unless you count putting two stripes of cream blusher up my cheeks and rubbing it in). And I do feel better. If I do the morning drop-off, I can talk to people because I am certain I have brushed my teeth before leaving the house.

It also means that when I forget I have a scheduled Zoom call for work, I can still take it, rather than cancelling it or hiding behind a chair as if they are actually in the room and can see the state of me. I feel more in control. I think it even has an impact on how I email. My working days at home are more disciplined and I'm certainly getting more done and not feeling bad when I stop.

And even better, I am surely a more effective role model for my children. Mary Poppins knows that you can't tell a child off if you are wearing pyjamas. You can't administer a serious bollocking in bare feet. It simply won't work (I have tried). However, if you are standing your ground in a pair of shiny leather boots, they will be more inclined to listen. I'm not suggesting you wear full military dress, but a decent outfit is a kind of armour in a wide variety of situations.

I see that now and I have made some changes. I don't know how I let myself slip so far from a basic standard. I have started to buy some new clothes where I used to not bother. I had two dress codes: 'work from home slob' and 'black tie event'. I had but one outfit to cover everything in between, including meetings, weddings and funerals, and that is not normal. Now I have 'professional, comfortable day wear' as a category and it has been a significant help. I have something to reach for in the morning. Sometimes I even lay it out on the bed before I get in the shower. My husband no longer says, 'Ooh, where are you off to then?' simply because I have brushed my hair.

What I found so comforting about Mary Poppins as a child was that she always seemed in charge of herself and therefore (to my young eye) everything else. She was never on the back foot. How I dress impacts how I feel and therefore how I behave. When Poppins tells Michael to 'Put your best foot forward,' she assumes the foot will have a decent shoe on it, rather than a sock that doesn't match the other one. How can I claim to be in charge of my household when previously I was clearly not in charge of my footwear? I hope I can see a new glimmer of respect in my youngest child's eye, but that may be the beginnings of conjunctivitis.

And it goes further than keeping myself tidy. I don't want to walk around in pristine cotton jumpsuits and understated yet impactful jewellery in a house that's a mess, so I also now make sure all the toys are tidied away at the end of the day. Then we can start afresh the next morning and this inspires you to keep going. It's not so much Broken Windows Theory, as Broken Toys Theory – if something's tidy, you're more likely to keep it tidy.

These things feel so embarrassingly basic when I write them down, but I lost sight of their importance. We tidy together and we even enjoy it (sometimes). There is no magic involved, but knowing everything is in its box, rather than just pushed to the edge of the room like a scurfy tide of plastic, means the evenings are more relaxing. Which can feel a little magical when you're not used to it. It's much nicer to sit with a glass of red wine in hand in a room that has been returned to 'adult state', once your progeny are tucked up in a clean bed, rather than swigging it from any clean mug you can find in a space that still feels chaotic, the echoes of the day's play all around and the threat of treading on a piece of Lego with a bare foot (the worst domestic pain known to man) ever present. It used to sometimes feel easier to fall asleep in the chair rather than have to navigate through it all. But no longer. It's neat and tidy. The mind is calm.

It all sounds so old fashioned, I know. But I have seen in my own living room that things can slide into something a bit too casual that ends up being exhausting for everyone. Because if there's one thing Mary Poppins excels at, it's boundaries. The example she offers provides a way to preserve the magic of childhood (jumping into a chalk painting, for example) whilst also maintaining standards. I aspire to this more than anything, even if to have both magic and order going on at once takes some sort of genius. As writer, broadcaster and *Mary Poppins* fan Victoria Coren Mitchell says, 'As soon as I understood that this was a benevolent figure (which was pretty immediate), I liked the certainty with which she drew her lines. I try to do the same as a parent, though I'm not as good at it. And I have no access to a magical world, which really compensates for any sternness during the day. Nevertheless, it is my observation that my daughter's happier when she knows what's what, and that is something I distinctly drew from those books.'

I feel the same, and a few weeks of being a bit more conscious of my personal standards has given me some new and better habits. I'm not trying to say this is going to solve everything, but the Poppins Doctrine of seeing a problem, setting a boundary, and taking action can be helpful in beginning to clear up some mess that is getting you down. Once the house is tidy, you can then address other areas of your life that are bothering you – perhaps some work you need to do elsewhere that you've been avoiding.

But the main point is that parenthood should not be a punishment. We don't need to try to do everything, to hold ourselves to an unrealistic domestic standard and then feel like a failure when we don't achieve it. But there must be a way to be imperfect but also practical, without losing your children or your sanity. I'm not perfect, I'm not even Practically Perfect. I still wear maternity trousers, six years after my last pregnancy. I do not think this will ever change, because when I first put them on I shouted in sheer surprise, 'FUCKING HELL, WHY DOESN'T EVERYONE WEAR

THESE ALL THE TIME?' and my enthusiasm has not since dimmed. But sticking to a few basic rules – upholding a few basic standards – makes all the difference. And after all, well begun is half done. At least I've made a start.

# Chapter 4

# Sister Suffragette

*I*t really is quite striking that the first proper scene in *Mary Poppins* is the song 'Sister Suffragette', sung by Mrs Banks. It is a risky way to begin a children's film – not many others begin with a celebration of a historical movement addressing equal rights, represented by three middle-aged women parading around a house. But it sets out its stall: this is going to be a film about women disrupting the normal way of things, the accepted and traditional way of things. Mrs Banks is right at the centre of that political upheaval, before Mary Poppins arrives as a force for change in her own home – Mrs Banks campaigns for it, but Mary Poppins inhabits progress in her entire being – she is an entirely independent and self-sufficient woman, answerable to no one, she does what she likes. They are a formidable pair. If Mr Banks finds Mrs Banks' anarchic energy too much to take sometimes, just wait until he meets Mary Poppins.

This is a playful approach to the ancient idea that women bring chaos to masculine order. In fact, the notion of chaos and order as represented by the feminine and the masculine is as old as humanity's desire to tell stories. And telling a story, incidentally, is the absolute epitome of creating order out of chaos. There are many ancient myths, legends, folk stories and so on that discuss creation, or birth, as a messy but necessary business assigned to the 'mother', with order then imposed by a masculine element from outside of nature.

Later, the Christian church started insisting on God the Father (formalising many of their beliefs in the fourth century AD), cementing the idea that spiritual order is imposed by a lone, omnipotent 'male' figure, while the chaos of creation and birth is channelled through the less frightening and altogether softer 'Mother Mary', which lets women off the hook for offering Adam the apple and being expelled from the Garden of Eden, so long as we behave in a demure and 'Madonna-like' way (although not *that* Madonna . . .).

Popular fascination with the 'feminine' as a force of nature goes in and out of fashion, though it has always been a consistent source of interest for academics and intellectuals. A German philosopher, psychologist and doctor called Erich Neumann, who worked from the early 1930s to his death in 1960, famously explored the idea that within the human psyche the 'feminine' is something to be respected, and that many even fear it. Neumann found the concept of the feminine to be mysterious and unknowable, chaotic and messy, but also immensely powerful and an agent for rebirth and change to the accepted order of things. He became quite well known internationally – a bit of a psychology and philosophy celebrity in his era.

His work would certainly have been in the ether in the late 1950s and 1960s as women's rights took centre stage internationally with what is now often called 'second wave' feminism. It feels like the time was ripe to start playing with powerful female forces, even for a company like Disney. Perhaps part of Walt's renewed vigour in pursuit of the rights to Mary Poppins (and his higher financial offer to Travers) in 1959 was as a result of his sense that some of the themes of Mary Poppins captured the zeitgeist.

It's also likely that P L Travers was aware of Neumann's work by the late 1950s. She was a great reader with a strong academic interest in spirituality, myth and religion, and would have been fascinated by his theories about feminine power. She was also a passionate student and disciple of Greco-Armenian philosopher and guru G I Gurdjieff, who combined the practice of yoga and Zen with his writings on mysticism, myth and fairy tale. Travers was serious about her study with him and later became a respected senior member of the Gurdjieff Society, helping to index their library. Given the extent of her reading, the overlap in interests and the contemporary nature of the work, it feels eminently possible that Neumann was on her reading list. If ever there was a time to finally bring Mary Poppins to life, to the screen and to a wider audience to explore her chaotic energy and her quest for some ultimate higher order via her feminine powers perhaps this was it. Perhaps Travers sensed that, too.

Now, *Mary Poppins* is ultimately a brilliantly entertaining film about families and children and the importance of being grateful for what you've got. But it is my belief that anything that endures in the entertainment world for more than 30 years has something else going on too. Something that speaks to deeper truths of the human experience. And *Mary Poppins* has all of that alongside the fantastic songs. It lightly picks up some of these ideas and plays with them, tossing them around, disguising them, turning them into lyrics and music and animated sequences and so on, but they are undoubtedly there. Underneath the showbiz, the message is clear and it's this: watch out men, here come the women.

We are in 1910 and George Banks sings proudly, and erroneously it turns out, that it's the 'age of men!' But it isn't. Because as we have just heard in 'Sister Suffragette', his wife, Winifred, has been going on protests and marches demanding votes for women, leaving her children behind in the care of another for the sake of what she sees as a greater good (and perhaps more fun . . .). His home is run entirely by women, to the extent that Mr Banks has very little idea of what is going on domestically. And finally, Mary Poppins, his new nanny, arrives on the scene, and where he expects to dominate and instruct her, she is defiant and even contemptuous of his understanding of order. He cannot understand how she can be in possession of the nanny advertisement written by the children; he mimes ripping it up and throwing it in the fireplace again and again, trying to understand what has happened while she gazes on, a note of pity in her eyes.

Which brings me to back to witches, which is traditionally where feminine chaos and the power of harnessing nature collides. Remember when I asked if you thought *Mary Poppins* was a story about a nanny or a witch? Poppins is 'feminine' chaos made flesh. The danger is that you'd never know it to look at her. She holds the magic inside her. There is no external indication that she has these powers – she does not need a wand or a cauldron or a book of spells. There is no sign of a cat. Instead of perching rakishly on a broomstick she travels decorously, feet together, under a very English plain black umbrella.

We know Poppins is anarchic and unpredictable. We know she has magical powers. She is also utterly in tune with nature – she can talk to dogs, she can duet with wild birds, she seems able to command the wind to bring her torn-up pieces of paper. We can be in no doubt that Mary Poppins is 100 per cent witch, whichever way you look at it.

I loved anything witchy when I was a pre-teen girl, hungry for ways to explain what was changing in my body and my psyche. The idea that I had some immense internal powers that were, as yet, unharnessed and could possibly control the weather made perfect sense to me. I would take books out of the library that were full of spells I could try. I felt a special shiver of anticipation if magic was spelt 'magick' – in my feverish imagination the addition of a 'k' to the end suggested a higher level of authenticity. I read all I could about Wiccan practices. I fancied myself a witch. I wanted a coven. I tried a love spell. It didn't work, but I put that down to novice teething trouble and being repeatedly disturbed by the dog. Then I found Jesus at the age of thirteen and suddenly I wasn't allowed to be excited by it any more – my church was very strict about anything it considered to be part of the 'occult'. Hallowe'en was banned. They didn't even like chiropractors (true story).

In fact, the very thing that led me to walk out of my church forever – the straw that broke the camel's back insofar as my faith was concerned – was the attempt, led by the vicar, to ban *Harry Potter* when it was first published in 1997. We were all required to sign a petition against it. I refused. It was noted (by the vicar rather than God himself, I assume) and I soon found myself dropped from various positions of responsibility (although this may also have been to do with me eating more than my ration of biscuits when helping with the tea and coffee service . . .).

The irony was that my evangelical church was engaged in its own magical beliefs – I was involved in and witnessed at least a dozen 'exorcisms' during my time there and also saw people who claimed to have been instantly physically healed of long-standing illnesses. There were many who said they had had their lives turned around in the space of an evening, having been made 'free' of decades of drug and alcohol addiction. There were others who had suddenly seen that there was more to life than just work and money and had subsequently reconnected with their families. Just like George Banks, actually. In this respect, Mary Poppins is doing the same work as the church, but in better clothes.

I think this idea of being independent and possessing a kind of private power was one of the main things that appealed to me about witches as a child and it is an appreciation that has grown stronger as I have aged. Later in life I have picked up my adolescent interest and when I attended an exhibition on witchcraft at the Ashmolean Museum in Oxford a couple of years ago, I saw that I am not alone in my enthusiasm. It was packed, mostly with women, poring over the items on display, including a very creepy silver bottle with a waxed stopper, which, according to folklore, contained the trapped spirit of a witch. We all walked around with mysterious smiles on our faces, drinking in the female energy and trying not to frighten the men with any sudden movements.

Witches are, in 2020, having a bit of moment, so I know there are many more out there who share my interest. The phrase 'witch-com' (in place of the far blander sit-com or rom-com) has entered common parlance among TV makers due to the massive upswing in pitches being made by writers that feature a witch at the centre of the action. I even pitched one myself. One company said they already had three separate witch projects in development. And of course, all this also coincides with the 2018 sequel to *Mary Poppins* itself, starring Emily Blunt in the title role.

Why the sudden witch love? There seems to be an outpouring of fascination for stories of this specific type of female power, now more than ever before. It's partly that the emergence of feminism, the economic independence of women, the right to vote, the right to own property and so on, not just in the West, but more recently and more slowly in other parts of the world, is leading to a new interest in what is really going on inside those of us who call ourselves 'women'.

But there's more to it than that. A gathering of witches is of course a coven, where powerful women meet to share, compound and amplify their strengths, which is either magnificent or terrifying, depending on your point of view. I'm sure I'm not the only woman who refers to her most tight-knit core of female friends as her 'coven'. In light of all the recent scandals and revelations involved in #MeToo and other similar movements, is it any wonder that we want to explore and test the limits of female power, for both political and entertainment purposes? Women have started to take back the power. No one said it couldn't be funny too.

And all this is being helped by new streaming services such as Netflix and Amazon, who cater to a huge female viewing audience. TV is employing more and more women in key roles too, changing the face of commissioning, writing, producing and directing. Reese Witherspoon recently said that sophisticated data tracking newly employed by streaming services shows that the idea of a female lead being off-putting to audiences – which has in the past been pedalled as a reason why these shows don't get made so much – is wholly incorrect and in fact viewers of all genders are quite happy to watch a show with a female lead. She said this had totally changed her producing clout and her approach to new projects.

In the past, in a more male-dominated industry, witches were more often portrayed as frightening, bitter, jealous, ugly old hags who only have it in for the pretty ingénue. Walt Disney was as guilty of this as anyone – his succession of 'evil old step-mothers with magical powers' pretty much single-handedly gave us the visual reference for a wicked old crone. But in 1964, he did something new. He brought us a kind, pretty witch who only wants what is best for the children and seems able to charm any man she meets into submission. We will partially forgive him.

Mary Poppins was a new kind of witch back in 1964 and since then we have seen a steady flow of 'good witches', reaching its zenith in the last few years with a slew of shows where the central witch is relatable, attractive and, though sometimes misunderstood, is generally found to be a force for good – see the monster success of *Frozen* and *Wicked* for evidence. In fact, the writers of the hit song 'Let It Go' from *Frozen* have spoken of how they deliberately tried to provoke empathy for Ice Queen Elsa, even though she was originally written as the villain of the piece. The song was so good, the story was rewritten around it to give a more even-handed perspective of the two lead female characters and reduce the stark nature of the 'good versus evil' dichotomy.

These days we want to understand the witch, not hate her. Independent, complicated, educated women are no longer for burning. I live very near a site where, several hundred years ago, witch burnings actually took place. I often go out of my way to walk past it. There is a huge and healthy yew tree there now. Something about the air buzzes, though that could be my imagination.

Traditionally, in films or TV shows, there is an evil witch, sometimes countered by a good witch. They will fight for control of someone young and innocent. The most famous example is probably *The Wizard of Oz*. But in *Mary Poppins*, she is both the good witch and the central character and there isn't an evil witch for her to fight. The evil comes from capitalism and the neglect of family values. The foe to defeat is the rejection of freedom and spontaneity, too much love of money and other oppressive concerns of adulthood. So Poppins is not only a powerful force, but also a moral one. Her magic may be anarchic and chaotic sometimes, but the irony is that she is deploying it for good. That was new in mainstream entertainment in 1964. It's still pretty fresh in 2020, to be honest.

What I notice more than anything watching it now is that *Mary Poppins* is a film full of women who are following their own path. Poppins herself is a case in point of course – she literally goes where the wind takes her. But Mrs Banks is a role model all on her own, as are servants Cook and Ellen, who are a formidable pair not to be messed with. Even the old lady selling bird feed seems somehow at one with her surroundings, though that may be rose-tinted of me. Anyway, she makes it look quite appealing, unless you have a phobia of pigeons.

I loved Ellen the Maid and Mrs Brill the cook as a child, and do still, watching it now. Constantly at war, they never give an inch, but with good humour in their eyes. I am from their stock, from an ancestral point of view. There are some lovely artistic types in my heritage but mostly, from what I have cobbled together from the various family tree-type apps and websites, it is clear that I am descended from long lines of agricultural labourers and household staff in both the male and the female lines – broad and stout, with a thigh circumference that would rival any rugby player. I am the sort who lifts something heavy and people say, 'Blimey, you're strong.' In 1910, I would almost certainly have been an Ellen or a Cook, if I wasn't hacking away at wheat in Suffolk. The most I could have hoped for was running a pub somewhere and even then I would have been changing the barrels.

At the beginning of the film, Ellen and Cook are having a heated discussion with the departing nanny, Katie Nanna, about the whereabouts of the children when Mrs Banks bursts on to the scene fully flushed with vigour and excitement from her suffragette meeting with Mrs Pankhurst and the others. She is oblivious at first to the domestic chaos in her house, but when she does discover the children are missing and her nanny is resigning, she seems remarkably unbothered. She has her mind on other things. Her way of dealing with stress seems to be to assume everything will work out in the end, and she's right.

God knows the burden of motherhood falls heavy, and sometimes heavier than necessary, so do let's raise a cocktail glass to Winifred Banks for providing a representation of this hallowed and sacred state that is funny and satirical. I know she's not really a great example of a mother – for a start, she never seems to have any idea at all where her children are or what they're doing. So I'm not suggesting this is a way of bringing up children I intend to emulate, but nevertheless it's playful and seductive. And comic, too.

She stares at her children with such love and wonder, the way one might at a litter of kittens when you have absolutely no intention of taking one home. It's a type of motherhood that would be looked at in horror in today's more punitive atmosphere. But in *Mary Poppins*, she simply shifts the full burden on to anyone who is around and hopes for the best. It feels naughty in a delicious way.

It's a brilliant foil to the starched uprightness of Mary Poppins, even though Mary is also totally irresponsible in her own way. It feels like a relief, somehow. To see a woman, a wife, a mother, so unburdened. I sometimes feel that I have to watch my back, watch my words, even my thoughts and feelings in the world today. Feminism claims to support all women in our individual choices, but that hasn't stopped a consensus emerging that doesn't include all of us, however broad it may be.

The policing of how we live, how we mother, is subtler now than it was in 1910 but more pervasive. It plays on our guilt and starts before the baby is even born. The phrase 'concerned expectant mothers' appears with alarming regularity as we are pushed into more restrictive behaviours than ever, whether that's regarding eating a soft-boiled egg, a slice of Camembert, or even using a brand new frying pan. 'There may be no proven link between a new frying pan and birth defects but concerned mothers-to-be will want to be cautious.' Will we? Or will we just end up in a weeping mess in the corner, paralysed with fear and unable to do anything much without worrying whether the risk to life is so great that we should remain indoors at all times until the baby comes, lest we be accused of acting like an 'unconcerned mother'?

It's the most modern of straitjackets – put the responsibility back on to the individual, absolve yourself of all legal requirements, just slap on one of those awful stamps with the silhouette of a heavily pregnant woman in a red circle with a red line through it and have done. It even appears on bottles of wine. The first time I saw it, I had to stop myself from throwing it at the wall and I wasn't even pregnant at the time. We know not to drink to excess. We know that the odd glass won't be a problem. We know that those who drink heavily through pregnancy have serious medical problems with addiction and are not going to be deterred by a little symbol on a bottle of

Malbec, so what's it there for, really? To remind us that we're being watched and to tell us that if anything goes wrong it's our fault for not being 'concerned' enough? Leave us alone. So, it's glorious, just for a moment, to see the depiction of such a wholly unconcerned mother as Winifred Banks. And to see that it all works out fine in the end – albeit courtesy of a full-time nanny.

I also think that, even as a child, I understood that Winifred Banks is sexy. Whether she was *meant* to be sexy is another matter, but the fact is that Glynis Johns makes a Votes for Women sash look hot and there is nothing anyone can do to stop it. I smile at her now – she is so delightfully irresponsible and mischievous.

In fact, both Mrs Banks and Mary Poppins embody a sense of mischief that runs all the way through the film. I think 'mischief' is a highly underrated quality in both people and art and it does have a lovely witchy sort of quality to it – teasing and light. Sadly women are often called out for creating mischief, especially if the target is other women. When I was doing my sketch show on ITV, most of the characters I created, or the celebrities I spoofed, were women (although I did have a great time covering myself in homemade hummus whilst dressed as Chris Martin). When I did press interviews to promote the show, I was very often asked whether I felt that spoofing women was 'anti-feminist'. I know of at least one major female popstar who refused to meet me for an event because she said I 'hate women'. And I hadn't even spoofed her at all . . .

We should be able to tease each other. We don't have to pretend everybody is perfect to remain part of some ramshackle sisterhood. It doesn't have to be humourless. We don't have to act as if daring to suggest that a woman in the public eye is a bit annoying or has some questionable or hypocritical traits is 'hating women'. We don't have to go along with supporting every female politician even as she dismantles our human rights before our eyes, just because of 'feminism'. We can oppose it. We can satirise it. We can laugh at it, and by extension at ourselves. We can cause a little mischief.

That naughty glint in the eye that seems to run throughout *Mary Poppins* feels subversive to me now. I was surprised by this. I remember feeling comforted and entertained by it as a child, but there is also a challenge in it about acceptable ways to 'be' a woman.

I think Mary Poppins' total lack of sentimentality – which I find quite appealing – is another way that this is challenged. The film's portrayal of this is fairly consistent with the original books, though P L Travers still thought the Disney version went too far, adding more than just the one spoonful of sugar, against her wishes. But it is still a triumph for that no-nonsense attitude Travers loved. That breathtaking line at the end of the film as Mary is about to leave Cherry Tree Lane, 'Practically perfect people never permit sentiment to muddle their thinking,' calls out to me like a song.

If you respond with emotion, I'm finding, you will soon find yourself mired in it. It's exhausting. Don't show them your neck, that's what I say. Don't show weakness unless you want to. Share, by all means, but do it in a way that is controlled and will help you, rather than in such a way as to make you feel weaker than you were before.

I am not a fan of the lazy equation: 'emotional = feminine'. Sometimes keeping things inside has been a necessity for me, not least in my work where, as a comedian I have often had to perform when horrible things are going on behind the scenes – that's life, we all have to go to work. I'd be finished if I turned up and sobbed onstage because I'd just had some bad news or a row with a friend.

I've lost count of the times I've muttered, 'Pull yourself together,' at my dressing room mirror reflection and then gone onstage. It'll be the same for every performer you know. We are probably at the extreme end of the spectrum on this, and I'm not necessarily saying that getting up onstage and telling jokes is the best way to deal with personal difficulties, but it's reassuring to know you can 'pull yourself together' when you need to.

Generally, the concept of 'being a woman' or 'being feminine' is something I largely ignore until someone rudely reminds me what I am, often in expectation of thanks ('I've always promoted women in this industry') or in order to shut me up ('Shut the fuck up, you stupid bitch'). It gets tiring. When I was young, I was very unaware of my gender. Most photos from family holidays show me clad head to toe in blue – jeans, T-shirt, trainers, unbrushed hair, muddy. It was a struggle to get me into a dress. I was noisy and unabashed. I played the trumpet. And then of course I went into stand-up comedy, where I was – and am – often the only female in the room. I haven't designed it like this, it was just what I wanted to do, and I went crashing in full pelt.

I'm not always nice, or lovely about it – it's not always possible, though you can always be polite. Mary Poppins is always polite. But women seem to be under great pressure to be 'lovely' these days, no matter what they are doing, but I think I prefer loyal, efficient, professional, reliable, decent and honest. I'll leave 'lovely' at the door. Mary Poppins is not 'lovely', but she is all these other things, and the better for it. Mrs Banks on the other hand is 'lovely', and yet I wouldn't trust her with my keys, let alone my children.

Lovely is a construct. It's a way to make yourself small: 'lovely' women apologise a lot and they start emails with 'I was just wondering

. . .' or 'Sorry about this, but . . .' I have been this person and it takes up a lot of time; I resent the toll it takes on my energy. I love Mary Poppins because she just comes out with what she wants and then blinks at you whilst you work out what to do. As an adult woman watching *Mary Poppins* again now, it seems remarkable and revolutionary, even in 2020. Women should not have to be nice to get on in the world, just as men should not have to be aggressive. I'd rather be fair. I'd rather be firm. I'd rather be kind. Sod nice. Sod lovely. And I'll never explain anything again.

All the women in *Mary Poppins* are fun, full of authority and they don't take any shit. I think I imbibed a lot of this messaging as a young girl. Be any kind of woman you want to be – a feminist mother, a cocky nanny, a sassy servant, a witch. They are all unbowed. They are all utterly in control of themselves and uncontrollable by anyone else.

The film's final scene takes us almost back to the beginning with the image of Winifred Banks' Votes for Women sash tied to a high-flying kite, soaring above London. If it's a symbol of what is really going on here, then I, as a stout, imperfect, chaotic, mischievous, noisy, subversive, unfeminine woman, am all for it.

# Chapter 5

# Jolly Holiday

The famous and much admired animated 'Jolly Holiday'/'Supercalifra gilisticexpialidocious' segment is also the sequence that very nearly sunk the whole attempt to get *Mary Poppins* on film. For author P L Travers, the combination of animated, talking animals and her own beloved creation, Mary Poppins, was the horror that meant she couldn't possibly do business with Walt Disney. She said no to him for twenty years. TWENTY YEARS! I can't imagine holding out for more than twenty minutes if a huge movie mogul wanted to buy the rights to my work, but then, I have almost no principles.

Even when Travers saw the 'Jolly Holiday' scenes in all their glory, she hated them. There wasn't an awful lot she could do about it, however. Disney had given her script approval as part of the deal but not final edit approval, so contractually speaking he didn't have to run the animation past her. She sat in the cinema at the premiere and seethed. She found Disney afterwards and told him it would have to go. He uttered his infamous line, 'Pamela, the ship has sailed,' and walked away. They never spoke again. She hated it so much that when a producer later came knocking for the theatrical rights, she would only agree on the basis that no Americans could be involved in the creative process of writing a musical based on her work. That is a visceral loathing of dancing penguins so deep you can only admire it.

But she was wrong. In terms of entertainment value, at least. And the animated/live-action 'Jolly Holiday' section of *Mary Poppins* was a triumph – a technicolour explosion that lifts us into Mary's world. In her autobiography, *Home Work*, Julie Andrews talks about how the whole crew was feeling its way in the shooting of it, using cutting-edge technology that took months to perfect after the principal photography was finished. I find it fascinating that even though technology has now so far advanced to the point where you can bring real actors back from the dead to complete their scenes posthumously, these scenes don't look dated; they are still exciting to watch. The colours are still vivid as I remember them, the animals witty and charming, the little visual flourishes stylish and captivating as ever.

This is the first time Poppins really shows us what she can do, too, in terms of sheer transporting magic. The finger-snapping game where the nursery clears itself up is cool but this is of a whole different order. The former is a domestic chore spiced up a little with some sleight of hand, perhaps. This is straight-up fantasy. They jump into a flat and slightly vague chalk pavement painting and land in a detailed three-dimensional world. Suddenly we are far from the city, the colours are bright, the sky is blue, you can almost feel the warmth of a gentle breeze on your face.

The lovely thing about this holiday sequence being the first trip Jane and Michael take with their new nanny is that it reveals her priorities. Yes, they tidy the nursery first, but then it's time to cut loose and race some carousel horses. Poppins prioritises pleasure – she does this continually – whilst also managing to maintain an air of self-denial and control. She is clear with George Banks when she tells him she will take the job that she will have every second Tuesday off. There is to be no discussion. (In fact, in the original book she has an argument with Mrs Banks about it, who tells her it is more usual for a nanny to have every third Thursday off, but Poppins isn't having any of it. She is serious about her boundaries.)

When the moment comes to jump into the picture, she may roll her eyes and appear exasperated ('Why do you always complicate things that are quite simple?' she asks of Bert, after his own attempt at magic), but you know she doesn't mean it. She's planned for a diversion – it's scheduled in. If Mary Poppins holds it to be true that having a 'jolly old time' is an important part of the day, then I feel there's no harm in knocking off early every now and again and having a beer on the way home. The lesson here is have a plan, but don't forget to allow for some spontaneity.

A holiday, a night away, even just a stolen lunch in a local café (not literally stolen – always pay for your sandwich, reader, Poppins is watching). You're far from the cares of everyday life. On holiday, there is no cooking, no washing up – unless you make the fatal error of self-catering, where you simply take all the chores with you to a new place where you can't find anything and don't know how any of the stuff works and for some reason expect to feel more relaxed than usual. And I'm not even going to talk about camping, where you even have to build the accommodation yourself.

And you can always, shall we say, hope to 'refresh' your relationship on a break from home. Is it any wonder that Mary and Bert, in their pristine new holiday outfits, get a little more flirty than usual? Who wouldn't? Who doesn't get a bit sexy in the sunshine? Although, that said, it can also be a scary make or break moment for any relationship.

I spent literally years badgering a holiday-shy ex-boyfriend to go away with me. He always said, 'But you won't like me on holiday.' I thought that was ridiculous. And then I finally got my way and we booked a week in a beautiful beachside resort hotel in Morocco – the turquoise sea glinting and winking at us from our balcony; the finest dinner buffet I have ever seen; a private cocktail table by the hot white sand – and he spent the entire week, and I do mean the *entire week*, in our room with a wet flannel on his head, watching sports on his laptop. The relationship was over fairly soon after we got back. Though it pained me to admit it, he was right. I didn't like him on holiday. But I couldn't really blame him – he had warned me. I should have listened. He has a right to his kind of holiday, but perhaps best if he goes alone, or at least without me.

In fact, holidaying alone is one of the greatest luxuries on earth, as far as I'm concerned. I have only managed it once in my life but it will go down as one of my greatest. I even wrote about it for the *Guardian*. That is how strongly I felt about it. Though it was slightly awkward when my husband saw the headline: 'I had the greatest holiday of my life alone.' But I explained that it was before I met him and, in any case, you're never allowed to write the headlines.

I was alone in Egypt on New Year's Eve in 2007. It felt so decadent, to order a cocktail on my own, eat when I liked, read and fall asleep as I pleased. I think being a bit self-reliant is one of the best things one can learn, especially women. I have met so many who won't go out for dinner alone, who won't enter a party without someone to arrive with and who certainly wouldn't dream of booking a trip abroad by themselves. I wish that wasn't so. Honestly, all you need is a book. You don't even have to read it. Just take a book, put it down on the table next to you and everyone will instantly relax because it shows that you planned to eat alone. Waiting staff and fellow diners can stop worrying about whether you have been stood up and might burst into tears at any moment. No, for you have a book, all is well. It's like a magic trick.

And then you can enjoy yourself on your own terms. I feel doing anything alone like this is very Poppins. The air of utter self-sufficiency and total lack of shame she gives off about doing her own thing is 'goals', as the young ones might say. When she arrives back from her 'day off' to find that Michael Banks has been pulled up the chimney, there is no mention of where she's been, who she's been with, what she's been doing. You wouldn't dare ask. I always like to imagine she's been plotting with other magical nannies at an international summit, eating sugar-frosted rose petals, sipping rum punch and incubating further chaos. But who knows?

I don't mean to sound glib. It's not that easy to schedule in a bit of decadence and then keep to it. And I know I'm not saying anything revolutionary here, but I have certainly at times in my life denied myself these things for too long on the basis that I feel I haven't been productive enough to deserve them. Which in turn makes me less productive.

Anyone who, like me, works in a freelance capacity (and there's a lot of us about these days) or has to endure a zero hours contract against their wishes (and there's a lot more of you too), knows how hard it is to carve out time for holidays, or even just a bit of down-time, in advance. I have been freelance for twenty years now – my whole career and half my life – and so have never known what it's like to have a reliable salary. In that time, I have managed to book a holiday more than a month in advance on only three occasions, one of which was this year. All the others have been on a 'MY GOD I SO DESPERATELY NEED TO GET AWAY, I CAN'T EVEN REMEMBER THE LAST TIME I HAD A HOLIDAY . . . Oh, I'm free next week, I'll go then' basis.

This works fine if a) you're not bothered who you go with and b) you don't have children. But as soon as the irresistible force of wanting a holiday meets the immovable object of 'school terms', things get messy. And expensive. Oh lord, just so expensive. When I first saw the price of two weeks at a forest-based leisure park for a family of four during the Easter holidays, I assumed I was buying the chalet outright. And if money is tight, the annual holiday is the first thing to go. You tell yourself you can have a lovely time in the garden – make it really nice. Maybe even pitch a tent and have lots of barbecues. Freshen up the outdoor furniture perhaps? Get a couple of bay trees in lovely pots. Before you know it you're browsing 'cheap summer house for garden' on Amazon and end up spending more than you would have done on a last-minute deal to Tenerife.

Much of this is about confidence, of course. Which Mary Poppins seems to have in abundance. You have to look at the year ahead and say, 'No matter what, I will have those two weeks off,' and then stick to it. Or it never happens. You have to tell yourself you will not bring your work home and resist having that little peek at your laptop while cooking dinner. You have to firmly resolve that the work emails are going to be ignored all weekend. It's very hard to do, especially now people are in the habit of emailing at 10pm on a Sunday night, signing off with a jaunty 'No need to reply immediately!' Too fucking right there's no need to reply immediately. Judging by the contents of your email, I'd say there's no need to reply until at least Tuesday lunchtime, but perhaps that is why I am self-employed.

It sometimes feels like a lot of things that should be simple and fun have been turned into work by the creep of social media. For example, hobbies are turned into commercial opportunities in the modern world in less time than it takes to learn to knit. It used to be that you could go to a local fair or fete and some woman would be there with her mate, selling jewellery they had made from one of those craft kits you can buy in the shops. Or perhaps a couple who make fudge at the weekends and sell it every now and again in little bags. It was for fun, it wasn't meant to end up on *Dragon's Den*.

Now there will be a board on every stall with all the social media info, plus a feedback form and an invitation to sign up for the monthly newsletter. I don't want a monthly newsletter, I just want to buy some fudge to eat and then forget about it. It's become work, that's what I'm trying to say. Everything is work. It's exhausting.

Mary Poppins goes to visit Uncle Albert upon hearing that he has laughed himself high again (literally) and needs bringing down to earth. Of course, when she arrives with Jane and Michael, her natural sense of humour and mischief takes over and they all have such a good time they too float to the ceiling. But when it's over she won't hear another word about it. It's done. It was great, but it's over.

Sometimes I just want to see my friends and have a laugh without recording any of it for posterity. It seems almost shameful now to let a birthday gathering pass without a single photo or video taken and shared somewhere. It's as if you didn't really care you were there if you don't record it. I even feel like this about weddings. Even my own wedding. We had no official photographer and no one making a video. People drank themselves silly and danced like absolute nutters and, so far as I am aware, apart from a few nice snaps taken by a cousin with a very good camera at the start of the afternoon, it exists now only in the memories of those who were present, assuming any of them can remember it.

Sharing everything has become the new normal – many of us shared pictures of our children on social media almost without thinking, but how many of us (myself included) are having second thoughts? We were so excited with all our new technology, and our new babies, that we forgot all about the sweet concept of privacy, not just for ourselves but for toddlers who can't give their consent before video footage of them covered in their own poo, or eating a daffodil, or licking the cat, is halfway round the world. Some of the most viewed YouTube videos in the world, watched by tens of millions of strangers, feature children who can't even talk. And that's without all the self-imposed intrusion by those of us who should know better – adults posting end-less intimate videos of our underwear, our lunch, our oesophagus . . .

I shudder at the thought of explaining Instagram to Mary Poppins. Can you imagine it? This is a woman who threatens to call a policeman on a child simply because he wanted to talk about their exciting day in the privacy of the nursery. The idea of Poppins sharing #soblessed pictures of them all having a picnic in matching bright white linen, applying sunlight filters, photo-shopping her thighs and tagging #Bert #London #JollyHoliday is too much. The shame of the neediness would kill her first.

That said, who needs camera filters when you can create a glorious technicolour world with your own magic? Poppins curates a perfect English day (#perfectenglishday) for the Banks children – or perhaps Disney's idea of a perfect English day – combining oast houses, weeping willows by a stream, afternoon tea, a funfair, a fox hunt, a day at the races, and a music hall singalong with some pearly kings and queens. And also, penguins. I defy any influencer in the world to better that.

She even brings a new word to the scene –Supercalifragilisticexpialidocious. Initially it seems like something quite fun and innocent – just a nonsense word you can pull out when you're not sure what else to say. But as the song develops, we find that it has more powerful connotations. It is in fact a magic word. For, as Poppins warns us later in the song, 'Better use it carefully, or it could change your life.' An intriguing prospect. Is this her own magic word? I am thrilled with this discovery, this window into her secret world – it had never occurred to me before that this is a real word to her, something significant.

And in fact it turns out that there is truth in Poppins' warning, for though George Banks initially dismisses this nonsense, or his need for it ('Yes, well, I always know what to say'), he calls on its power when he is sacked at the bank. He pulls it out, he laughs hysterically. He shouts it to the rooftops. 'She's right – it does make you feel better,' he trills with glee and runs off into the night. Better use it carefully . . .

It's really no wonder George Banks has to let some of the tension out. He's been walked all over by these grand old men of the bank for years, it would seem. He is so nervous around them you almost want to stroke him. They have systematically destroyed his boundaries. And then suddenly, thanks to Mary Poppins and her chaos and nonsense words, and the subtle encouragement from Bert, he finds he has the vocabulary to throw off the weight of it all and find himself again.

'Having boundaries' is a relatively new way of describing the actions of a person with a decent level of self-respect. It is simply deciding what is and isn't acceptable to you, as an individual, and drawing a firm line between the two. Mary Poppins is one big boundary, as far as I can tell, upon viewing the film with a more modern, more adult eye. For example, her day off every second Tuesday is non-negotiable, she refuses to talk about things she doesn't want to, she reveals nothing of herself other than what she wishes to and she is completely unworried about being disliked even by her own boss, Mr Banks. She is outwardly inscrutable, despite all that riot of magic and energy going on just below the surface.

I've had a sharp lesson in the trampling of boundaries since joining Twitter way back in 2009. It feels like a hundred years ago now, but at the time it was in its first flush of success. It was a lot smaller and a lot chattier. There weren't really 'pile-ons' or twitch-fork mobs, and trolls still lived under bridges and required passwords to cross (they may still do that for all I know . . . they're anonymous online anyway).

It was a nice way to meet people, to make contact with someone you didn't know personally but had always admired from afar, or just shoot the breeze without fear or favour. We had a little group called the 'Ladies of Twitter' that comprised journalists, writers, presenters, sports stars, musicians, comedians and actors. There were about 30 of us. We even ALL met for dinner on two occasions, giddy with excitement. We would support one another, no matter what. The

Sisterhood had found its medium. It's no coincidence that at around the same time, Male Twitter, in the lumpen forms of Sir Alan Sugar, Jeremy Clarkson and Piers Morgan, were merely tearing chunks out of each other and willy-waving.

Then something changed. I do not know what, when or why, exactly, but in some respects it has become a monster. I suspect it has something to do with the arrival of the 'blue ticks', which made a hierarchy where once there was an equality of sorts. These ticks that appear by your Twitter handle don't mean anything other than the bots that crawl around the app have been able to verify with some external links that you are the person you say you are. That's it. There are no special privileges or powers. I have one, and yet there are people with more followers than me who don't. It seems to be completely random. But the ticks appeared to put some people on a pedestal, and being on a pedestal is not always pleasant, especially when not everyone is pleased to see you there. In fact, it drives some people mad. I was once told to 'take your blue tick and fuck off' simply for saying I liked spring.

I was in the first generation of women on TV that had to deal with Twitter abuse – the now familiar 'You're not funny/'You're fat'/'I wouldn't rape you with his' sort of brilliance. I would go on a panel show such as *Have I Got News for You* or *Never Mind the Buzzcocks* and I would enjoy myself at the recording, say a few good lines, hope they made the edit. Then the show would go out and you'd think I'd been murdering puppies on screen.

When the trolls first discovered Twitter, women got the brunt of it and we comedians came in for some vicious lashings. At the time, you would almost certainly be the only woman on a panel show, and an effect of this was that we never saw one another. We never really had the opportunity to talk about it as we rarely encountered each other professionally and we didn't want to share it online and so it became a dark and nasty secret. Does everyone else get comments like this, or is it just me? Do they all just brush it off; am I being oversensitive? We individually felt shame pricking our confidence. There was a sense of retreat, of withdrawal. Boundaries that were hazy and poorly defined went up as a reaction to fear, or disquiet. I could feel that my performance on these shows was becoming quieter, more polite, to try to avoid abuse later. Sometimes I would feel a smart remark, a retort, or some political joke flash in my mind but decide not to say it, not to take the risk. In other words, I watched my mouth, and trust me when I say I have never previously been known for watching my mouth. If something felt a bit sharp, I blunted it before it could do any harm, even though it meant I came across as bland. I don't think any of us quite knew how to handle this new world we seemed to have blundered into.

Now though, there are far more women working in comedy; you might even get more than one on the same TV show. This was a dangerous prospect when I was starting out in 2005 – producers were perhaps nervous our menstrual cycles would sync if we sat next to each for too long, creating a hormonal tsunami in the studio. Such fears were unfounded as we managed to create space for ourselves, and so there's a new generation of women in comedy that are great in number, talent and confidence.

Taking a good long look at Mary Poppins has led me to rediscover some of my own lost confidence – I want to keep fresh in my mind that image of her, standing on the Banks' stairs, looking defiant, saying incredibly firmly, 'Let me make one thing quite clear: I never explain anything,' before marching off, leaving George Banks gaping and helpless. And she has also reminded me of my desire for fun. Because I have realised that I have not made space for that enough in the last five years.

I used to be good at being decadent. In fact, I was so pleased with myself about my work/life balance during my twenties, I remember piously telling someone older than me (they were probably the same age I am now, with that familiar weighed down look I see in the mirror sometimes these days) that, 'Laughter, sex and dancing are all you need for a long and happy life.' What an annoying thing to hear from a twenty-year-old twit when you are feeling old and tired, and there's still a lot to do before bedtime.

But I have realised that I still think there is some truth in it. Laughter is infectious – it's good to laugh well and laugh often. A good solid belly laugh will do anyone the power of good and I challenge any doctor to disagree with me. Mary Poppins spends a whole afternoon with her guffawing, airborne Uncle Albert, singing 'I Love to Laugh' and it doesn't add a single thing to the story other than an infectious sense of joy and fun – these are her priorities, no matter how stern she may pretend to look about it.

So I am going to follow her lead and try to re-engage with my more decadent self. I will carve out more time for straightforward, un-taggable fun. I will stop replying to work emails on a Sunday night or when I'm out with my son on a Saturday morning, I will not respond to anyone who is abusive on Twitter, particularly if they have fifteen digits after their name and a picture of Hitler (or more usually a dog in a football strip) as their avatar. My time, and my mind, will be my own again. For if there's one thing Mary Poppins won't do, it's waste a minute of her life on anything she doesn't think is worth it. Sometimes the outside world feels frightening, politically unstable, menacing and serious – particularly in recent years. But even so, there has to be a way to find levity. More than find it; insist on it. Every second Tuesday, as a bare minimum.

Chapter 6

# A British Bank

It is wrong to be 41 years of age and still fear your post, I know it is. And yet here I am, stuffing another fistful of envelopes underneath a large coffee table book about Elizabeth Taylor's diamonds. It hides them very nicely, it's lovely to look at and it makes me feel much better about my own profligacy. Any envelope that appears to be from a financial institution holds a particular terror. I have never dealt well with money. It seems to desert me from the moment it arrives. I am simply unable to hold it down. It calls to me to spend it.

As a teenager, my monthly pocket money was a perfectly reasonable amount for a new top or two but I always figured that it would go further if I spent it in charity shops. And it did. I would come home with armfuls of musty second-hand clothes that had seemed like a good idea in the shop but, once I laid them out on my bed, I could immediately see I wouldn't be seen dead in any of it outside of a convention for devout Mormons. It was an immense waste of money.

One of the reasons for the existential terror around money is that my grasp of numbers is limited. Words I can handle – I was taught to read by my grandmother before I even started school. She was a remarkable woman by the name of Violet Brand. A literacy pioneer in her time, she was one of the first to develop phonics as a spelling method, became an expert in dyslexia and was later awarded an MBE for her work. And she used me as a kind of guinea pig when she looked after me, which she frequently did. I basically got one-to-one literacy teaching, using all the most cutting-edge theories, by a renowned expert in her field, before I was even five years old.

Violet was very Mary Poppins in her outlook too – never complain, never explain. She had a battery of little Poppins-like aphorisms at her disposal, such as such as 'sharp's the word, quick's the action' or 'neither a borrower nor a lender be' and there was something a bit magical about her too – she hid old sixpences in a homemade Christmas pudding and claimed a dark ring of grass on her lawn was a 'fairies' circle'. She never, ever ran out of roast potatoes. And she wasn't particularly interested in money, except to give it away.

Thanks to her wonderful teaching, I developed a level of confidence around words that was unusual for my age and for that I am grateful because if I had to rely on my maths ability to have a career, I would almost certainly be in prison by now. Numbers are not my forte. I find them mysterious and tricksy and difficult to control. They always seem to get away from me. Mathematical tuition can enter and then leave my brain so fast that I would defy any physicist to explain it. Anyway, to cut a long story short, I eventually scraped through GCSE maths to the immense relief of my teacher and walked away from this mad language of numbers that I could never really grasp.

But a deficiency with figures is a practical problem in life, which, added to a 'money burns a hole in my pocket' character flaw, means my finances are always in peril. I remember once, when I found myself short of cash within 24 hours of being handed my allowance and nothing much to show for it, my father patiently explaining the Micawber Principle, named for Charles Dickens' insolvent clerk in *David Copperfield*. It reads thus: 'Annual income twenty pounds, annual expenditure nineteen pounds nineteen shillings and six pence, result happiness. Annual income twenty pounds, annual expenditure twenty pounds nought and six, result misery.'

I nodded along, fully comprehending the message, vowing to be better. And here I am, the best part of 30 years later, and not much closer to living by this simple rule. Do not spend more than you earn. Easier said than done, for me at least.

My problem is that I get a bit high from spending money I don't really have. And when I am terribly broke, which I have been many times in my life, I get the overwhelming urge to spend my last bit of cash on something wildly stupid and pointless. It's almost a pathology. I once spent the last £20 I was going to have for another month on a meal in a local restaurant which consisted of a very overcooked duck breast served with raspberries, broccoli and black beans. It was as disgusting as it sounds. On the walk home, I calculated that I could have fed myself reasonably well for the next fortnight if I had spent it in the local grocery shop. At the Edinburgh Festival one year, I ran out of money a week before the end. I had £10 to keep me going. What did I spend it on? A cinema ticket to see *Wild Wild West* starring Will Smith. It was so bad, I left after twenty minutes and walked back to my shared, rented hovel, again calculating all the things I could have bought that would have been more sensible.

What is wrong with me? I do not know. I can only defend myself by saying I am equally loose with it when I have a lot of it and I spend it on other people too. I am also eternally optimistic and when I have had terrible quiet periods with work that have dragged on month after month – year after year in one instance – I like to employ that other Micawber-ism: 'Something will turn up.' And you know what? It usually does. But the wait can become so nerve-shredding, I have questioned whether it's worth it.

I really must grow up now, though. I want to grow up. While living like this is all very well when you are in your twenties and can last a day or two on Diet Coke and Frazzles and sleep on a sofa if you really have to, you can't do that once you have a family to support.

Once I had children to look after, a previously forgotten event called 'lunch' re-entered my life. This was a wake-up call. It was not enough simply to have a box of Crunchy Nut Cornflakes in the house and a pizza for tea. Children expect to have another meal in the middle of the day and they will not be fobbed off with wine. And this means you must actually go shopping at regular intervals and buy substantial amounts of food each time. And this requires money. I'm sure none of this is a shock to you, dear reader, but it was to me.

And even more sobering is the thought of living like a student when I am in my dotage. What may be charming at 22 is rightly considered a little pathetic at 72. I don't expect great luxury, but neither do I wish to be tapping up a friend for 50 quid or pretending to have left my purse at home when I meet someone for a coffee when I am old. It's not a good look. And so, I must engage in a more responsible fashion with the bank. I need to look at my finances without wincing. I need a . . . pension? I need . . . investments? I need to pull myself together.

The evils of capitalism are not lost on me. It would be very nice to live in a system where I could rely on a bit of government support during dry periods, global pandemics notwithstanding, but the days of casually 'signing on' for a couple of weeks for actors or writers are long gone. I watched *Withnail and I* and loved it, but the part I did not understand was when they got some dole money because their agents hadn't called. I went into my local Job Centre in my early twenties when some promised TV work did not materialise to enquire about temporary benefits until something else came in and was met with a stare of incredulity and incomprehension. You do not get dole money for not being able to find acting work these days. You go and work in a restaurant and beg for time off for auditions until you either get an acting job or you end up managing said restaurant.

And I'm not suggesting the latter is necessarily a bad thing. The industry can't sustain the number of people who want to be actors or writers and that's not the government's fault, and it's certainly not the fault of hard-working, tax-paying people in jobs they do not love. I don't expect to be funded while I fail at something so wholly inessential as this – not that the arts as a whole are inessential, mind, but rather my personal contribution. The thing that is both great and terrifying about working in the creative industries is that no one is going to beg you to carry on if it's not working. If you give up, someone else will be along to take up the slack. There is no shortage of talent. If you stop paddling, you dip below the surface, the waters close silently over your career and, in a year or two, you are forgotten.

It nearly happened to me. Only bloody-minded determination and an immunity to humiliation saved me as I trudged back to the Edinburgh Festival in 2016 with a stand-up comedy show to perform in one of the smallest rooms available. It was a do or die moment. I had no idea if anyone would even turn up. But it worked. And I lived to fight another day. But no one was begging me to work. If I hadn't done that show, my career was all but over and I would have got a job at a garden centre perhaps, and then later featured in a *Daily Mail* article about how this 'former comedian was down on her luck and now selling tulip bulbs from a lay-by on the M40'.

My trouble is that although in one sense I could leave maths behind at GCSE, the fact is that being smart with money is about being smart with numbers. It's about understanding risk, calculating percentages, balancing books. The only balancing of books I understand is making the pile of unread ones on my bedside table structurally sound so they don't fall on my head while I'm sleeping.

It was OK when I was being given pocket money in cash – I knew how much I had and I knew when it was gone (usually within 24 hours). But once I had a proper bank account, and with it a student credit card, the wheels came off almost immediately. Interest rate percentages were not something I could grasp very easily. The first time I went abroad on my own I had a terrible time with currency exchange – I could never work out which way round you calculated bought and sold money. I only had 'divide by 10' in my head from the time I went to Paris with my school in 1994, which was the rough difference then between French francs and British pounds. By the time I left university, French francs didn't exist any more and there were intimidating decimal places everywhere. Currency, exchange rates, credit agreements and the world of finance in general – the world of George Banks – was and still remains a total mystery to me.

George Banks works at the cold and imposing Dawes, Tomes, Mousley, Grubbs Fidelity Fiduciary Bank. It's an unapologetically adult place, with polished wood, vast high ceilings, pale marble floors. Old men walk around dressed head to toe in black, long tall hats like undertakers, speaking in hushed reverential tones. It is a temple, a place to worship money. We couldn't be further from the joy and spontaneity of the nursery or any day out with Mary Poppins and Bert. The contrast is striking. You can feel the chill of the place coming off the screen.

Had George's esteemed place of work actually existed in 1910 it would have been at the forefront of a new and developing world. Though no doubt it would have been a mystery to most ordinary people back then, as perhaps banks still are (holding my hands up here), so I am in full sympathy with young Michael Banks when he makes that fateful trip to work with his father, is spun some highly suspicious colonial nonsense about railways in Africa and decides to reject it in favour of keeping tight hold of his tuppence. Because when it all sounds like gobbledegook designed to relieve you of what little money you already have, you will only really put your faith in what you've got in your hand right now.

'Give me that and I'll turn it into more' has never cut much ice with me. It sounds like a con. It is a con. It's just it can take time for the con to reveal itself. Which it did in 2008 with the catastrophic banking crash and the realisation that when the computer says no, the biggest and most emphatic no in the history of digital banking, the numbers scramble until they mean nothing and we are left with empty pockets. Which makes me think Michael Banks was right, because it appears no investment can really be made 'patiently, cautiously, trustingly' in any financial institution. Better to buy a bag of crumbs from an old lady to feed the birds. And possibly the old lady herself.

This is one of the most subversive elements of the *Mary Poppins* story and a glimpse of the politics of Mary Poppins herself. It is she who plants the figurative seed in Michael's imagination on the eve of his visit to the bank with his father. She sings the most hauntingly beautiful song in the film and fires up his conscience to the extent that when he is confronted with a group of old men grasping for his money, he cannot make the leap to see why anything they suggest could be worth anything to him. And he does not want his tuppence yanked out of his hand and put somewhere he can't see it based on some dubious promise of semi-annual returns of an unspecified amount.

I too would rather have my cash under the mattress than in any theoretical form of numbers that could vanish at any time. I am a financial Luddite, a dunce. I know some people who work in the financial sector and, though I may like them from a social perspective, I do not understand them, nor do I understand what they do when they try to explain it. They are like another breed. Their brains work differently to mine. I do not entirely trust them, in the way that perhaps a dog doesn't entirely trust you to throw the ball once you have dummied it and hidden it behind your back for LOLs. I'm not saying they are bad people – many are extremely generous, charming company. But making money out of money seems odd and frightening to me. Like a magic trick where endless 50-pence pieces are seemingly pulled from my ear in a never-ending chain, when I know there is only one 50-pence piece simply being moved around to make it appear legion but I can't quite see how it's done.

The world of high finance is a con trick that we have all bought into and now somehow keeps the world turning. And when it stops, everything grinds to a halt with it. I would be more comfortable if we still traded in things I can see or taste, such as rock salt or opium, but apparently there's no going back now. We have created a system for ourselves that has locked us in. And in *Mary Poppins* we see modern banking at its birth.

But of course, its history goes a lot further back than that and no doubt this forms part of George Banks' pride in being part of an ancient and venerable institution. The first type of 'banking' as we may vaguely understand it in the UK started during the reign of Henry VIII when the dissolution of the monasteries led to goldsmiths accumulating gold that had belonged to the Catholic Church for the royal treasury. The storage and management of this gold meant that a new type of organisation had to be founded to keep track of its whereabouts and its value.

By the reign of Charles I, the Royal Mint was heaving with gold, but a lack of trust in the monarchy meant that aristocrats and other wealthy types wanted an independent group of goldsmiths to take their own gold and give them running cash to hold against its value. The gold standard was introduced to help regulate its worth – this set the price of gold. which was then used as a reference when valuing paper currency. The English Civil War led to demands for a new bank that was independent, an entirely separate entity from the royal treasury, and so away from the greedy and grasping hands of the king. In 1694, the Bank of England was formed.

Over the next 200 years, other, smaller, private banks begin to pop up, offering banking services to middle-class people and broadening what they could offer their customers, such as overdraft facilities and sales of bonds. These were often run by families and many joined together becoming partnerships, the names of which we would still recognise today – Barclays being the longest lasting and best known, along with Barings and Rothschilds. With the explosion of industry and global trade, new merchant banks and investment banks grew to fund economic activity overseas, particularly for countries with far-flung colonies such as Great Britain.

And so we can assume that by 1910, George Banks' place of work was a combination of all these trends; the lyrics of the song sung by Mr Dawes Sr to young Michael about where his tuppence will be invested certainly confirms the centrality of the empire to the world of banking. The list goes on, detailing railways in Africa, dams across the Nile, ocean-going ships for trade, and plantations of ripening tea. It is the first sign of a true global economy, an economy of oppression perhaps, funded by individuals such as Michael Banks putting their money in the bank and then enjoying the returns on their investment as the new projects pay off.

And that's a great idea, until it all goes wrong. Like it does in *Mary Poppins* and like it did in the 2008 banking crash that we are still recovering from. Because the one thing any financial institution dreads is a 'run on the bank'. All the money is theoretical – they don't hold everything they owe us in one place, such as the sixteenth-century goldsmiths might have. There's just too much of it and the same money is being passed from investment to investment, on the basis that not everyone will want their cash at the same time. Like the magician with his never-ending 50p, the trick only works if I never look him in the eye and ask to see all the 50ps at once. We both pretend there's loads of them because it suits us to believe it.

But Michael Banks isn't buying it. He has a tuppence in his hand right now. Dams across the Nile mean nothing to him. And what's more, he's been told a lovely story about an old woman who sells bird feed on the steps of St Paul's Cathedral, for only tuppence a bag, and this sounds like a much sounder investment to him than a plantation full of boring tea, thousands of miles away. And so he starts to yell that he wants to keep his money, sparking a panic amongst all the other banking customers in the hall and at the cashiers' desks and they too suddenly start demanding their money. The shutters snap down, chaos ensues, the children run away and George Banks gets his hat bashed in and loses his job. It is amazing how fast the veneer of civility drops away the moment rich people think their money is under threat.

But from where did this bit of Poppins mischief arise? There are several interpretations of the song 'Feed the Birds'. The first is literal, of course – you buy some crumbs to support the livelihood of a humble old lady and also feed the pigeons, which is a nice thing to do. It's also pleasant and enjoyable for you. I remember feeding the pigeons in Trafalgar Square as a girl, buying small bags of seed from people wandering around selling them. And as I say, it was a nice thing to do, until a whole flock of pigeons landed on your head and shoulders and crapped in your eyes and you left crying and in search of a cake to cheer you up. Then it was established that pigeon shit gave you meningitis and the whole thing was banned. Shame.

The second interpretation is that this is a song about feeding the little ones in your life with love and attention, that this costs little (just a metaphorical tuppence) but it means a lot. This is aimed by Mary Poppins at Mama and Papa Banks, who are both essentially ignoring their children at a crucial time in their development. By concentrating all their time and energy on campaigning and work respectively, the days are slipping by and they are missing out on family time they will never get back. This is the central theme of *Mary Poppins*, and it is all encapsulated in this song – cherish the simple things you can do with your children, feed your little birds, take time to care. This was Disney's view – he told the Sherman Brothers that this song was the 'heart of the whole damn thing'.

There's also a third interpretation which is more closely related to the subversive point about money that *Mary Poppins* is making – namely that we should use it to help others directly. We should not walk past someone trying to make a humble living, or hungry birds in need of crumbs, and instead try to swell our own coffers with obscure investments. And in fact, worse than that, not all these investments seem particularly ethically sound, so you shouldn't just look away. In addition to the morally troubling funding of the colonial system, Dawes Senior lists other ways of making money through the banking system that might make many of us cringe – 'Foreclosures! Debtor Sales! Bankruptcies! Opportunities!' he crows. It's pretty distasteful stuff and not something you can imagine Mary Poppins approving of, given her friendships with the more artisanal and disenfranchised members of society, such as street artists, chimney sweeps and . . . small, slightly judgemental dogs.

In the light of the financial crash we lived through just over a decade ago, this message feels particularly pertinent. In 2008, it was found that financial products were being sold to people who simply could not afford them, using contracts full of jargon they couldn't understand, designed to offer rewards and opportunities that looked too good to be true, and were. People were sold mortgages on zero interest, or even negative interest, meaning they were being paid to buy a house. Some bought several properties on this basis, and these were not people with millions in the bank, or even steady jobs. They accumulated cheap debt but there was a sting in the tail. For the contracts had five-year terms, after which a huge hike in interest would kick in, making the repayments totally unaffordable to these individuals.

When agents and bankers sold these deals, they buried this detail in the small print, never bothering to point it out. Hasty signatures were procured and the time bomb started ticking. Then, once these debts became 'bad' or 'sub-prime' they were packaged up and sold on to other debt collection companies, who sold them on and sold them on. They were never going to be paid off; eventually no company would touch the debt and individuals went bankrupt, as sometimes did the banks that had signed off the loan in the first place. Someone asked to see all the 50ps and the whole mess exploded in our faces.

A handful of people got very rich by getting in and then getting out at the right time. A smaller handful made money on the misery in ways too clever, or nefarious, for me to really understand no matter how much I read or watch about it. Everyone else fell apart. They lost their jobs, or their homes, or both. We are still recovering.

I once did an interview with the *Sunday Times* for the 'Fame and Fortune' column, in which I was asked about all my best business decisions and my cleverest investments. I had to explain that I don't think I've ever knowingly made a business decision at all, unless you count buying a second-hand campervan that I thought I could live in if it all went tits up. And anyway, that then failed its MOT and I couldn't afford the massive bill to fix it, so I gave it away free to a man who agreed to tow it back to his garage. As for investments – the biggest investment I have ever made was a giant bar of Dairy Milk and there was very little return on that, unless you count an equally giant stomach ache.

I'm crap with this stuff. I'm not saying I'm proud of it and god knows there have been times in my life when I wish I was better.

But I think ultimately, ideologically, I'm with Mary Poppins and Michael Banks – keep your money where you can see it and spend it on things you can see and touch, and that might help others directly, too. I know this means I will never be rich. I know this means my financial situation is unlikely to improve because of anything clever I have done. But that magic 50p is just one 50p – I know it, you know it, they know it.

As well as teaching me to read, Grandma Violet showed me how to appreciate the small things. Her favourite activity with her grand-children was feeding the ducks at the local park. She liked taking very short train rides for no reason and, no matter how senior or important she was, I never saw her anything less than thrilled at the offer of a chocolate biscuit. She seemed to me to be a happy woman.

I think this is exactly the point of view that *Mary Poppins* is advocating. When business becomes so complicated and technical, so stressful and high stakes, and so removed from what we really need as humans, then we lose all sense of perspective and it becomes almost impossible to stand still long enough to value the things right in front of us. P L Travers talked often of the 'miracle of the everyday', which is about taking a moment to enjoy the simple things around us. Once the basics are covered, when we know we can put food on the table and pay the bills, then get out. Literally get out of the house. Go for a walk in a wood full of bluebells, laugh with a friend, admire a wonderful view. Fly a kite.

# Chapter 7

# A Man Has Dreams

*T*here is a brilliant moment in *Mary Poppins* where George Banks is delivering yet another lecture on how to run a well-ordered home as his house is literally falling apart around his ears. Thanks to the regular blast from Admiral Boom, the piano is sliding across the room, to and from his fingertips, eluding his grasp. He appears oblivious. He just keeps talking. It's funny but it's also a nice visual metaphor for what is to come.

Later, as the rest of his world crumbles, we will see George Banks brought down, humbled, confused and broken. His heart-rending scene with a soot-covered Bert in the drawing room, where he glimpses for the first time what he is missing out on by alternately ignoring and dominating his children, always leaves my mouth dry and my eyes moist. Through Bert's compassionate eyes, you suddenly see a different George Banks – he is sad, introspective. He admits in his part of the song 'A Man Has Dreams' that he feels regret for his own lost ambitions and unmet needs. You can only hope there is, with some help, at least the potential for a happier and more relaxed man.

You may not expect *Mary Poppins* to be dealing with a theme that feels so modern, but issues of 'toxic masculinity' – a phrase that's come into usage recently to describe a set of circumstances, social expectations and pressures that are no longer considered helpful or healthy to the wellbeing of our menfolk – are right in there, depicted in the character of George Banks. In fact, you could say it is the driving force of the whole film. For me, one of the most touching scenes in *Mary Poppins* is when Bert explains to a tearful Jane and Michael that their father needs them, because he has no one to talk to about his feelings.

There is a quote attributed to American poet and philosopher Henry David Thoreau that says, 'Most men live lives of quiet desperation, and die with their song still inside them.' Is this true? It feels a tragic admission if so, and it wrenches the heart. I have quoted it to a handful of men over the course of my life, some introverted, some gregarious, some successful and some disappointed, and they always look stricken, go a bit quiet and mutter something like, 'Blimey, that's a punch to the gut,' so I apologise to them, and wish I hadn't said it. But these similar reactions from men who outwardly at least seem very different would seem to confirm that these words still carry a sad resonance. I have so many fabulous friends who are men – kind, sensitive, supportive, funny. I have known some of them to struggle with their mental health and I have sometimes struggled with how best to offer help without causing offence or inflicting further blows to already fragile self-esteem. Looking around me, I wonder if perhaps I am of an age where some men of my generation – and certainly the one above – still suffer at the hands of this idea of the 'stiff upper lip', that most toxic legacy of the patriarchy.

George Banks is certainly clinging to his sense of order and propriety in a world that is changing too fast for him to keep up. He is rigid. He is pompous. He believes that 'Life is a battle to be faced and fought.' At the film's opening, we are shown a man who recognises no room for whimsy, fun or spontaneity. When we first meet him he is on his way home after a hard day's work at the bank. We, the viewer, have just seen the utter chaos erupting in his home but he is blissfully unaware. Already he is on the back foot, even as he marches jauntily along with that P G Wodehousian air of 'God is in his Heaven and all is right with the world.' He sings of his pleasant life, his deep satisfaction, his slippers, his sherry and his pipe. He expects order. He expects to be in charge. He cannot, at this point, possibly know what is coming for him.

As I watch *Mary Poppins* now, the story of George Banks hits me with fresh significance and relevance. His journey over the course of the film is undoubtedly the steepest and the most dramatic. In essence, despite Poppins being the nominative hero, this is the story of George Banks and his salvation. It is how he is taught by fair means and foul to value his children, his family, his free time and, perhaps most importantly, himself. Because even though George Banks thinks he is in charge of everything, it's only when he loses it all he sees how precarious it is. And then he starts laughing at the absurdity of it all, goes missing for a night and emerges a man with a smile on his face and an appreciation of letting go.

Of course, there have been many social changes since 1910 – many of which were ushered in by the campaigning work of Mrs Winifred Banks and her sister suffragettes. These days, many women who work suffer under the pressure to balance family and career. But with that acknowledged, I feel that it is appropriate to devote some time to the message the film carries for men in particular. As has been well documented over the past decade or so, we are in a time of mental health crisis for many men. Suicide is the leading cause of death for young men in the UK; many in the public eye and out of it are bravely speaking up for the first time about the loneliness and isolation they feel that leads to despair and self-destruction. What this has highlighted, among other things, is that everything George Banks would have believed to be right and proper at the height of his pomp in fact can also be experienced as a cage closing around you until an existential moment of panic and anxiety becomes a way of life.

Toxic masculinity teaches young men, starting when they are boys, that they should not express emotion; they should not engage honestly with those around them; they should be brave, fearless, ambitious, ruthless; that intimacy, gentleness, humility is a sign of weakness. And many in the media continue to collude with this fiction. Even James Bond (all right, Daniel Craig) cannot carry his own baby in a papoose without being abused for being 'unmanly' by that paragon of human understanding and empathy, Piers Morgan.

Watching George Banks grapple with his sense of duty and responsibility as Mary Poppins arrives in his home and starts throwing his idea of order out of window is both funny and poignant. Played to perfection by the masterful David Tomlinson, he manages to show how a man can put down his defences and find another way to live. At the start he is pomposity itself, so sure of himself, dominating his wife, his children, his staff. He barks at them, he patronises and condescends, and they take it, even women's rights campaigner Mrs

Banks (though with that naughty twinkle in her eye). But Mary Poppins is not any kind of woman George Banks has encountered before, and so his re-education begins. She breaks him and then she starts building him up again.

Does he deserve it? Possibly not. He's a decent sort – a bit of a prat, but he loves his wife and kids and he is a man of his time. Does he need it, though? I would argue that he does. He is lost, doubting himself perhaps for the first time within a few moments of her arrival. All that confidence of Empire, of being an 'Englishman' and master of all he surveys, the king of his castle, simply evaporates almost as soon as she produces the ripped-up piece of paper with Jane and Michael's advert written on it, that he himself tore to pieces and threw into the fireplace, and stares him right in the eye, gently mocking, totally unflinching. She will not be patronised. She doesn't even allow him to interview her properly, only implying she will take the job if she wants it, not if he offers it.

At this point, George Banks seems laughable and unsympathetic. We want to see him brought down a peg or two and he has it coming. His overbearing behaviour towards his household, to the 'women' he clearly finds to be silly and irrational and the children who must be dominated and overruled, is unappealing and begs to be undermined. Remarks about the household being dominated by 'slipshod, sugary female thinking' are not terribly endearing. But it is gently done. And carefully. Poppins is never rude, just firm. Women like this do not exist in the world of George Banks.

Banks tries to fire his new nanny after she returns with the children from their riotous afternoon tea with Uncle Albert, but yet again he is thwarted. She will not allow it. She is not done with him yet. Instead, she tells him that he is taking his children to work with him in the morning and that is the end of the discussion. But what starts as a comical and satisfying takedown of this man becomes something much more complicated. What P L Travers seemed to want, and to his credit what Walt Disney also understood, was to handle this male ego delicately, even kindly. Yes, he is humiliated, but there must be redemption.

George Banks' look of total bewilderment, his sense of losing all contact with land now he is very much at sea – perhaps this is where Admiral Boom comes in, to try to warn him of the incoming bad weather – marks a change in the film, taking us into the final act, which is really all about this man. It stops being a fun film about a magical nanny and her naughty charges, and the seriousness of its real theme, its true message, takes hold. And that message is that there may be men in your life who need help, and if they can't help themselves because they don't know how to, someone may have to step in. Mary Poppins is not just a nanny to Jane and Michael, she is also there to shepherd their parents too.

Much of the last third of the film takes place in the bank and therefore in the life – I'd actually go so far as to say the *psyche* – of George Banks. In theory, the professional man we have seen singing oh-so confidently about the 'tradition, discipline and rules' embodied by the exalted institution that is a British bank should be in his element here. But this is where the film does something quite clever.

Mr Banks arrives at his venerated workplace with his two children ready to teach them important things about banking. The partners appear, travelling in a pack, seeking out Mr Banks, who now seems nervous for the first time. You begin to worry for him, though you are not quite sure why. But he seems vulnerable somehow. And any parent who has ever had to take two outspoken, slightly unruly children to the office with them will feel his pain as the boss approaches. Though he is proud to show off his children to his colleagues, and vice versa, it feels like his confidence is faltering, somehow. And then it all kicks off for real and he doesn't have a clue what to do. There is panic in his eyes and we have stopped laughing at this pompous, self-satisfied man.

After they flee from the bank, the children are rescued from the scary back streets of the East End by Bert. In many respects, Bert is the most 'maternal' figure in *Mary Poppins*. He exhibits his emotions gently but freely. He talks about how he feels and displays immense empathy towards everyone. He is kind to the children, explaining the complicated adult world to them in terms they can understand. Where Mary Poppins is all action and crisp practicality, Bert is soft and compassionate. He always seems to have time to listen.

It is Bert, this wandering man of no fixed employment or abode, who is able to open up the emotional inner life of Jane and Michael's seemingly distant father to them for the first time. Almost as if he has a children's book with pictures and flaps you can pull back, Bert shows them what it's like to be a man like George Banks. For, as he says, 'I always observe that a father can do with a bit of help.' He goes on, 'Who looks after your father? When something terrible happens, who does he talk to? No one, that's who.' The pressure, the responsibility, the loneliness is gently revealed. Jane starts to cry. They both do. So did I. And here it is, one of the most beautiful exchanges I have ever seen:

Bert:  You know, begging your pardon, but the one my heart goes
       out for is your father. There he is in that cold, heartless
       bank day after day, hemmed in by mounds of cold, heartless
       money. I don't like to see any living thing caged up.

Jane:   Father in a cage?

Bert:   They makes cages in all sizes and shapes, you know. Bank-
        shaped some of 'em, carpets and all.

Well, ain't that the truth. And the possibility of saving poor, pompous old Mr Banks from himself emerges. The children will do it. There's no one else who can. It's touching because we can see that it is the moment for Jane in particular where she grows up and starts to see her father as a human being, with vulnerabilities and pressures. And it will be his children's support that allows George Banks to glimpse another life.

The parallel of this scene is the lovely, lyrical 'A Man Has Dreams' number close to the end of the film, where Bert has a bit of a man-to-man chat with George Banks, who knows his job at the bank, along with his status in the eyes of middle-class Edwardian England, hangs in the balance. Bert is diametrically opposed to George in every way. He wants no part of the patriarchal system, he goes where he likes, he does what he likes. He owns nothing, but he owes nothing. He has a sense of loyalty and decency but he doesn't seem hemmed in by it. George, by contrast, constantly seems to be trying to push the lid back on a boiling pan of water. At some point, he is going to have to give in and let the steam escape. It's coming, it's coming. Perhaps Bert and George represent the two sides to every man.

There are some beautiful sentiments in 'A Man Has Dreams', wrapped up in such delicate lyrics that are half spoken, half sung, which adds to the sense of emotional honesty. Bert's words to Mr Banks are gentle and so full of empathy that it makes me a little tearful just to think of it. And so Bert is able to reach a deeper part of George

Banks that others have not – or perhaps have assumed is not there. And it seems to make an impression on Banks, who still sees Poppins as a dastardly outsider but is warming to this soot-covered stranger in his drawing room. But Bert is on Mary's side here and therefore on the side of the children. He thinks they need their father in their lives, and not just to bring the money home.

But, as seductive as it is, such an emotional approach still sounds strange to George Banks – rooted as this character is in this portrayal of 1910 establishment masculinity – though he is undoubtedly curious. Bert's words are making some kind of impact here, but George Banks has yet to learn his full lesson.

We can see that a change has started to come over George Banks when his children hand him the tuppence that had caused so much trouble – he knows it won't help him make amends for his transgressions in the brutal world of capitalism but instead of saying so, he takes the coins and gravely thanks the children. He leaves the house and walks alone to his fate like a bowler-hatted René Magritte painting, sauntering facelessly away from the camera, anonymous in the rainy, low-lit park.

His total degradation by his colleagues when he arrives at the bank is hard to watch. But then, something miraculous happens; as he bumps to rock bottom, he finds some kind of freedom in it. And he has a word – that magic word. The word that you had better use carefully or it could change your life. 'Supercalifragilisticexpialidocious!' He yells and then he's gone, back out into the night.

On the face of it, it's a total disaster, but somehow you know it's not. Because surely now he knows there's something to come home to that is more than just a well-run, orderly house, with everything and everyone put away in cupboards or behind doors by the time he gets there, so he doesn't have to confront anything he can't handle. In fact, he has two children who love him, a wife, a real home. It's not too late to participate.

Something I had forgotten until I re-watched the film was the reference to suicide. The next morning, the Banks family have no idea where George is and they are all worried. Ellen makes a joke about 'dredging the Thames' and, when he turns up, Winifred clasps her husband and says, 'Oh George, you didn't jump in the river – how sensible of you.' Of course it is done with a comic touch, and what we now think of as inappropriately offhand references to suicide are hardly rare in films from this era, but it still made me jump a little. Because it does happen, and we now know that suicide is the leading cause of death for men under 45 in the UK. It is not intended as a hugely serious moment in *Mary Poppins*, more an expression of their concern and relief at his return, but it still serves as a reminder of the stark reality behind the words.

But happily, our George Banks is home safe and seems unaccountably well and happy, given what has happened to him. He finally sees that life can be messy and chaotic. Mary Poppins shows him this. Some men seem to find this very difficult to handle, and it must surely be because when something is messy and chaotic it may provoke a messy and chaotic response. And men are still taught that they must keep control of themselves in a very particular way – that it would be weak to cry or even to acknowledge that something has gone wrong.

A good friend of mine once told me (after quite a lot of red wine – it was that kind of chat) his view is that life is random and disordered and unpredictable, and so are people. So you have to adapt your behaviour *ad hoc* – there is no moment the same as the last. People's emotions change from second to second and a remark that may have gone down well with a partner last week might for some reason cause offence this week. One of the greatest skills a person can have is to read the room, and this means being attuned to people's emotions. To some extent, women are trained to do this from birth, being told to smile in the street or give someone a hug to cheer them up. Reading the emotions of others can be a survival skill too, helping a vulnerable person in a tricky situation to size things up quickly and act accordingly, possibly changing tactics. You have to be adaptable and flexible.

And yet it seems to me that sometimes men are at a disadvantage socially because they are often taught that rules are the most important thing, however you're feeling. Lay down a series of rules which have to be kept to all the time; do not deviate from them whatever is happening in front of you. Circumstances may change but the rules cannot bend. A rule is not the same as a boundary. Boundaries come from within, from a place of self-knowledge, but a rule is imposed. Living under a system of rules that are not fit for purpose when humans are always changing only causes tension, frustration and anger. Mary Poppins has boundaries. George Banks has rules.

The success of people like Jordan B Peterson, the controversial philosopher, men's rights activist and bestselling author of *12 Rules for Life: An Antidote to Chaos*, is not that he gives out especially original advice ('Tidy your bedroom and make your bed in the morning' is straight out of *Mary Poppins*, his most ardent followers might be horrified to learn) but that he helps young men who feel lost in a world that is random and often without logic feel that they are in charge again. And this is destructive because it only perpetuates the lie. The key is not to try to wrest back control of everything – your bedsheets perhaps, but not women, or the ongoing march of equal

139

rights, or the changing employment landscape – but the opposite. As Mr Banks is shown, the key to finding some peace is to give in to the chaos sometimes and see what emerges.

Obviously this is easier said than done. But if you try to keep controlling everything, you will find yourself in a lonely place because it's hard work, it's usually futile and it makes it much harder to ask for help, as to ask for help is to admit that you have lost control of a situation. If you press on regardless, you will end up lonely and exhausted, and that's horrible. In the most extreme cases, it is debilitating and dangerous. I do not wish to dance on anyone's misfortune, and I feel no glee or satisfaction in this, but I do not think it is a coincidence that Peterson ended up seeking medical help as he was suffering anxiety connected to a dependence on opioid painkillers. There is a problem and it appears his is not the solution. I wish him better.

I also don't want to sneer at Peterson's success because he is important to a lot of young men who feel baffled and abandoned, but I do think it is a tragedy. I was stuck on a train recently and struck up a conversation with a nice young man opposite. He was doing a maths PhD and we chatted for a while about that and the fact that being stuck on trains was an increasingly regular occurrence for both of us. Then he asked me, completely out of the blue, if I had heard of Jordan B Peterson. He seemed surprised that I had. The young man was a fan and keen to outline Peterson's theories of life, the universe and twenty-first century masculinity. I said I was not a fan and outlined some of Peterson's theories on forced monogamy.

There was a bit of quiet after that and perhaps a sniff of tension. Then he said quietly, 'I didn't know about that. That doesn't sound good.' And I felt bad, because I live in the same world he does, which means I have been socially conditioned since birth to not upset men too much – even if I am disabusing them of a prolific and wealthy vlogger and lifestyle guru's moral standing, and trying to explain everyday sexism, without sounding like a stuck-up bitch and exactly the sort of woman they are encouraged to hate. Sadly, we didn't get on to Mr Peterson's use of lobster society to explain why we should be more like the patriarchal crustaceans, so I never found out what he thought about that. I avoided the topic, but maybe that was shellfish of me.

What I'm saying is that this was a nice guy and he had found some comfort in the everyday common sense of making your bed in the morning, tidying your environment, clearing your mind, respecting yourself and others, working hard, being the best you can be. My point is that this doesn't then have to naturally lead to enslaving half the population for the sexual gratification of the other. Mary Poppins manages it and, in the end, everybody wins, even the bad guy. In fact, the bad guy is totally redeemed and becomes the good guy in the end. It's a better story to tell.

The train started moving again and we reached our station. We got off and said goodbye. 'It was nice to talk to you. It was interesting,' he said as he walked away. And I wished we could have kept talking, actually, because I wondered if I was the first woman he had had this conversation with. I wondered how women are spoken of generally on the Peterson fansites he possibly visits, because I've seen some of it and it's not pretty. I have thought of him sporadically since. I hope he's OK. I hope he's out and about talking to women, finding out what we know, and how we feel. I hope he gets his maths PhD. He seemed soft, and vulnerable somehow, and impressionable, like any 24-year-old.

I knew that there are many men who love *Mary Poppins* but I realised that I didn't know what the appeal is for them and if it differs in any way to what it is for me, so – in another utterly scientific study – I put a call-out on Twitter for fans of the film who identify as male and I got a huge response. I followed up to see what they loved about the film and whether there was anything in particular they could identify with.

Many men came back and said that they loved it as children because of the magic and the dancing, but as adults they can now see themes that they relate to more. One told me that in the absence of a big brother figure, he turned to Bert, who seemed free and cheerful. Another said that he wanted to be Bert as a child but had recently realised he had inadvertently become George Banks. One of the loveliest responses was the way in which some said they drew parenting advice from Mary Poppins herself. I think this shows how much more hands-on fathers are with their children these days. I bet if I had asked this question ten years ago, there would not have been much of a response.

Comedy writer Andrew Dawson told me:

> *'I sing "Stay Awake" to my son pretty much every night. I never appreciated how smart it was when I was a kid. I just liked the tune. But the reverse psychology of the lyrics set to a perfect lullaby melody is so clever for bedtime. So neat and simple. You're singing to them the exact words they want to hear, while they unwittingly nod off. It's perfect. Mary Poppins*

*in a nutshell. She's getting the parenting done, yet the kids still feel she's on their side.'*

The men are very sympathetically rendered in *Mary Poppins*, perhaps more so than the women. They are more emotional and less rational in some respects, which I think is a big part of the film's durability and charm. It seems unusual for a work that firmly falls into the 'family entertainment, domestic setting' category to have so many male fans, and I do wonder if this is partly because of how the male experience of life is represented – not just in the polar opposites of George and Bert, but also Admiral Boom, a comical creation, but also a raffish maverick figure who follows his own code and will not be quietened down for anyone, and Uncle Albert, who cannot contain his joy at the world but then weeps himself down to earth with Bert.

In fact, only the men cry in *Mary Poppins*. And all of the main men cry at some point. Even the formidable Dawes men, father and son, at the bank, are willing to show more emotion and vulnerability than is usual for 1910. And Dawes Jr is so impressed with George Banks' breakdown that he actually decides he is more of an asset than a liability, flings his kite skyward and offers the man a promotion.

All the men are redeemed. They all achieve wisdom in their various different ways, whereas the women are generally unchanged. At the end of the film, they know all the same things they did at the beginning – they just had to hold fast and firm until the men caught up. Even Bert, the most enlightened of the lot, has to stand back and watch Mary fly away, gazing at her departing form, gruffly muttering the words, 'Don't stay away too long . . .' Though he has no control over that and doesn't seem to ask for it.

The story of *Mary Poppins* is soft on the men, giving them the benefit of the doubt sometimes, and is all the better for it. If there was ever a film that shows us that the patriarchy is bad for everyone then surely this is it. I don't want to live in a world where men are frightened of themselves, or unsure of how to be around women, their children or a washing machine.

I think we've all come to understand that mental health is something that needs to be discussed openly and frequently, and there isn't enough help around for anyone – but statistics indicate that there are risk factors that are specific to men. Can I recommend *Mary Poppins* as a small cog in a whole complicated machine? Any man who sees the truth of the message of the film – that we all suffer under patriarchal social constraints and should throw them off as far as possible – will be enriched by it. George Banks crying, realising that he is more than his suit and his job, more than his mortgage and his own expectations of manliness, as his children approach to try to wipe his tears, is a beautiful image. I wish all men could see it; I wish fathers would watch it with their sons. I'm glad many have told me that they have already. It's a wonderful film about the pressures of being a man and the ways in which we can all help.

# Chapter 8

# The Life I Lead

By all accounts, Pamela L Travers was not a woman to be trifled with. She was determined, stubborn and could be extremely rude if she felt backed into a corner. She was formidable in many respects, combining ambition with a sharp intelligence that she embellished with a wide-ranging programme of reading and self-education. She was fiercely private to the point of secrecy and was happy to be awkward if an arrangement was not to her liking. And yet she also created one of the most enduring, whimsical, magical and enchanting children's characters of all time, introducing the world to Mary Poppins with her first book in 1934.

Travers loved stories. She told stories about her own life from early on in her career. Some might even call them lies. One entirely inaccurate story about her upbringing on a tropical sugar plantation in Australia was widely held to be true and quoted in several newspaper profiles of her during her life. In fact, much of her unhappy childhood was spent in a dusty rural wilderness. She liked to create new realities for herself. If the world was not to her liking, she imagined a new one. As she said herself, 'There are worlds beyond worlds and times beyond times, all of them true, all of them real, and all of them (as children know) penetrating each other.'

What is a story? Where do they come from? And why do we tell them? These may seem like childish questions but the answers are deep. Humans have a profound need for stories as a way of making sense of a world that can often seem random, cold and chaotic. Myths, folklore, gods and demons pepper the ancient heritage of every culture on the planet. We have fairy tales, witches and goblins to present moral dilemmas and play out our worst nightmares in a safe environment. The stories we tell our children when they are young can shape them as much as any real-life event. We remember our origins through story, we educate ourselves, we entertain one another, we even send messages. You could argue that a developed sense of story, of narrative, is part of what makes us human. It's not just telling tales of the divine; it makes us divine.

Strange, sometimes disturbing and utterly compelling stories were a huge part of my childhood. As I have said, courtesy of my grandmother, I was able to read by myself from an early age and could therefore enter all alone dark and glittering worlds that fired my imagination. Or I could pick up something light and free. I could alter my mood with the right story – a Roald Dahl for an unsettling ride, an Enid Blyton for some sturdy reassurance. But it was something I had for myself, something I could retreat to. Reading will give you a sense of power and privacy as a child that will never leave you.

Aside from books, my sister and I also had access to an immense bank of some of the weirdest stories ever created by way of a weekly publication called *Story Teller*, which began in 1983. Every Wednesday, my dad would bring a new one home. Each magazine came with a cassette tape with around a dozen stories on it. They were by turns wild, wonderful, funny, dangerous, amoral, sweet and downright bonkers, all drawn from folklore, fairy tale, and some original creations. 'Gobbolino the Witch's Cat', 'The Great Big Hairy Boggart', 'The Snake and the Rose', 'Boffy and the Teacher Eater', 'The Marog from Mars' and 'Warrior Girl' are some that I remember even now, 30 years on. They were read by people such as Floella Benjamin, Joanna Lumley and Brian Blessed. There were hundreds of stories and then a second series came bringing even more. It was a fabulous treat.

I couldn't get enough of them. I would listen to them all day. We would have them on in the car on long journeys. They have reached into my soul. I think the moral ambiguity and the sense of danger are the things I remember the most. As a child, I found it terribly exciting that sometimes the plan went wrong or the hero did not survive. I would stand by the claim that the two series of *Story Teller* tapes are the greatest collection of children's stories ever made. I think they have contributed significantly to my world view. I would recommend them to anyone, though getting your hands on them can be tricky, sadly. Most of our family tapes have been consigned to the great 'Where did that end up?' black hole of family history.

I didn't know they were pure gold at the time, I just knew I loved them. When I had children, I wanted to share them again, so I went so far as to buy the complete set from eBay. It cost quite a lot of money but I feel so glad to have them. I have started transferring them to a more modern MP3 format. They must not be lost to time. These stories are important – they taught me a great deal about life, as all good stories can.

Travers believed this, too. She wrote an essay called 'The Fairy-tale as Teacher', in which she passionately argues that myth and folklore of all kinds should have a place in our lives. She says:

> '*I have heard parents declare that they did not want their children to read fairy-tales for fear that they should grow up into wishful thinkers. [But] the fairy-tale can set up a chain of questions that will only take truth for an answer. One can hardly imagine a process less encouraging to wishful thinking!*'

Travers was convinced that the world we see around us is not the only reality and sometimes we have to be open to a greater truth – one that can be told with a story.

Travers' interest in myth led her to Greco-Armenian philosopher, G I Gurdjieff, whose influence on her life was physical (she talked of taking his yoga tuition to ease her anxiety) as well as intellectual. As Valerie Lawson describes in her biography of Travers, *Mary Poppins, She Wrote*, 'Through [Gurdjieff] she had learned more, and wanted to know more, of Zen . . . she had already been told that her Poppins adventures were "full of Zen", an idea which intrigued her more than any other theory.'

So Travers liked discussing ideas, she was quite spiritual and I suppose when you look at it, there *is* a kind of Zen energy around Mary Poppins. She certainly never seems worried or surprised by anything. If Zen is do with exercising self-restraint and trying to gain insight into the true nature of things in order to benefit others, I can see that these are all present in Poppins, even if Travers only learnt of it after she had created Mary. No wonder she was intrigued. Travers was immersed in this philosophical world of study with Gurdjieff and his followers by the time she signed the deal with Disney in 1959 and it seemed to be teaching her that there was a therapeutic element to her study of myth. That she was looking in the right place for some kind of deeper truth. Perhaps it enabled her to finally take more of a 'Zen' approach to Disney.

It seems impossible, given all this, that Travers was unaware of the work of American philosopher and academic Joseph Campbell and his own theories of myth and story. He was working during the same period and his analysis of human folklore *The Hero's Journey* was gaining recognition. He studied the nature of story and its inner workings. His most famous work is *The Hero with a Thousand Faces* (1949); in it he detailed how all the most successful and enduring stories in history come down to one essential set of ingredients and one archetypal hero. He called it the 'monomyth' and argued it underpins much of our shared belief as a human species, coming back time and again in myths, folklore and fairy tales. Of course, this single story can be told in a thousand different ways, hence the title of his book, but when you strip each one back, he argued, they always come down to the same essential component parts.

Campbell is also often credited with the line 'follow your bliss', though he says that he got it from Hindu doctrine and also a novel called *Babbit* by Sinclair Lewis. In *The Power of Myth*, Campbell quotes from *Babbitt*, saying, 'Remember the last line? "I have never done a thing that I wanted to do in all my life." That is a man who never followed his bliss.'

The realisation of looking back over your life and becoming aware that you have 'never done a thing you wanted to do' may be crushingly prescient now as a warning for many of us as we rush around completing our duties and chores, trying to please everyone and keep everyone safe. It's easy to forget what we originally wanted for ourselves. It is a horrifying thought – the idea that you could reach the end of your life having managed not do the things you wanted to do at all – not even one thing – and I think this was something that undoubtedly haunted P L Travers, whether she was directly aware of the *Babbitt* quotation or not. The idea that a man has unrealised dreams that are crushed is a very central theme in *Mary Poppins*.

Born Helen Lyndon Goff, Travers grew up in Australia, moving to England later in life. Her parents were troubled. Travers loved her father with all her heart and, by her own account, they were very close when she was a small child – he had a great imagination and imbued her with a sense of creativity and wonder. But he had a problem with alcohol and, after losing his job, he moved his family miles away from everything that was familiar and went to work for a bank – a career to which he was wholly unsuited. He became a shadow of himself, caged and miserable, and, eventually weakened by years of drink and disappointment, he succumbed to an early death. He was gone by the time Travers was seven years old. Her mother later attempted suicide by walking into a lake. She saved herself at the final moment, but the knowledge of it left a deep impression on her daughter.

It doesn't feel like too much of a stretch to think that – though refocused through the lens of a children's story – there are elements of her own father woven into the image of *Mary Poppins'* Mr Banks. Travers' need to tell a story that would somehow rectify the wrongs of the past was strong. In fact, there is an argument to say that anyone who feels a compulsive need to create stories, to shape narratives, is trying to correct something from real life, to shape it, to bring it under control. And it's not something that is confined to professional writers – it's a natural human instinct; in many ways, we all try to restore order by bending real events into a created story arc in order to control something that feels otherwise beyond our ability to solve. In other words, if we can't have a happy ending in real life, we can make one in a story, in our imagination.

I asked Emma Thompson what she thought, having researched Pamela Travers and played her with such sensitivity in *Saving Mr Banks,* a film which tells the story of the deal struck between Travers and Disney, interwoven with scenes of her early life. Emma said:

> '*I think Mary Poppins [was] created precisely to (unconsciously) put right and control the chaos and pain of childhood. Ronald Dahl also had a very painful childhood. Great children's writing tends – I think – therefore to come from writers who are dealing with their own trauma. Life isn't controllable – story is. We take the jigsaw pieces of life which make no sense and never add up and you can never find that last straight bit of skyline that will finish it all – and story takes the pieces and puts them together in a lovely ordered way and then puts a frame round them so you can step back and look at it from a distance. That to me is what storytelling is all about. Framing life so we can get a grip on it. Otherwise there is only the moment and you can't grip a moment. Although god only knows we try to.*'

Many have speculated on where Mary Poppins came from – I don't mean the character herself in the story, which as we know is a mystery that cannot be solved. But from where, within Travers, did she conjure her? Travers has said, with a slightly defiant tone, that Poppins didn't come from anywhere, she just appeared one day to her, as if by magic. And in some respects that's probably true. Writers hate being asked where they get their ideas from because, in truth, we don't really know – it is a mysterious process and trying to explain it can often feel like cutting open the goose that laid the golden egg, only to find there are no more eggs inside and we have destroyed the mechanism by which they are created.

But it is still useful and interesting to think about where a character as enduring and popular as Poppins might have emerged from, and Emma Thompson has some thoughts on that too:

> '*She was the creature that could put things right – wittily and without getting too involved. And then she went away. Mary Poppins is a sort of Western for children. The situation is chaotic and painful – the outsider arrives to put all into order using unorthodox methods and then MUST LEAVE, which makes everyone sad and happy at the same time. Pamela never had anyone to make things better for her. She had a confused and painful childhood and was a very difficult adult – albeit a marvellous friend.*'

This idea of *Mary Poppins* as a Western for children is a brilliant insight into what makes the character so popular nearly 100 years after her inception. And it also ties in with some of Joseph Campbell's theories about modern myths and the perennial hero's journey story that comes up in Western storytelling over and over again.

Of course *Mary Poppins* is not a Western, strictly speaking – it is not set in the frontier lands of the American West in the late nineteenth century, there are no cowboys, no 'Indians' and there are no guns. But in terms of the ever-appealing notion of the mysterious stranger who rolls into town, gets some shit done, shows everyone how to be a decent, stand-up guy and then rolls out again, it fits the bill nicely. And this idea that the hero 'MUST LEAVE', as Emma puts it, is very compelling. A happy ending doesn't always involve everyone staying together. Sometimes there is a higher justice at work, a call that only the hero can hear and has to answer. The wind changes and, for some reason, Poppins must move on. She is a loner who has some other purpose of which we only get a glimpse; her horse may be a talking parrot umbrella but still she hitches herself to it and is gone before anyone can say thank you. She is John Wayne in a floral hat and a pair of hob-nailed boots.

Travers may have claimed that the character of Mary Poppins simply appeared one day in her imagination but she also suggested that Mary may have been at least partly inspired by an aunt who came to stay with the family when she was a child. Helen Morehead, or Aunt Ellie as Pamela knew her, was practical and not emotionally fragile or needy like Travers' parents. Travers did create at least one character based on Aunt Ellie, who she called Aunt Sass, in a private semi-autobiographical book she gave to friends for Christmas in 1941.

And she realised what she had done, because in 'Aunt Sass' she even writes, 'I thought to myself, some day, in spite of her, I shall commit the disrespectful vulgarity of putting Aunt Sass in a book. And then it occurred to me that this had already been done, though unconsciously and without intent. We write more than we know we are writing. We do not guess at the roots that made our fruit. I suddenly realised that there is a book through which Aunt Sass, stern and tender, secret and proud, anonymous and loving, stalks with her silent feet. You will find her occasionally in the pages of *Mary Poppins*.' This was seven years after the first Mary Poppins book was published. Perhaps it took her a little time to realise for herself what the origins of Poppins were.

Although this autobiographical work started life as a private endeavour, with just 500 copies made for Travers to give to friends and family, in 2014 it was published by Virago. As a side-by-side comparison with the Mary Poppins books it is instructive. We can draw a line from Poppins, to Sass, to Ellie. These are organised women, rational, caring but not in a way that leaves the person being cared for exhausted by the emotional needs of the carer. And, as Travers says of her creations, they are 'secret and proud'.

Travers herself could be described as 'secret and proud'. And also perhaps 'anonymous and loving'. She longed for children of her own, but it was not to be, at least not biologically. It is possible she was gay, or bisexual, but this has never been confirmed. She had a few short relationships with men over the course of her life but she settled with a woman named Madge Burnand and they lived together for nearly a decade. This too came to an end and Travers decided to adopt a baby boy from Dublin, whom she named Camillus. He was one of twins – his brother was also adopted by another family, a fact Travers concealed from Camillus. He only discovered the truth when aged seventeen he received a mysterious knock at the door of his home from a man who wanted to talk to him. Travers chased him off but Camillus followed and went to find him in a pub. On walking in, he recognised his own face in this stranger and the story Travers had weaved around their relationship came crashing down. Until this point, Camillus had no idea he had been adopted. The shock was immense and their relationship suffered.

But there is no doubt that, in her own way, Pamela had been a loving if eccentric mother to Camillus and eventually they reconciled. He speaks warmly of her in a filmed interview he gave after her death but it is also clear that she remained a mystery to him, as she did to all her friends. She was not an easy woman, but she was loyal, interesting, and great company when she wanted to be. She was well read, curious, forthright, independent and indefatigable. Much like Mary Poppins herself. Perhaps she became her own Poppins, as so many do when they need something more than they were given.

I like adventure stories more than I like stories about emotions and relationships. I like stories where things happen and the emotions come with us along the way. Yes, people change and new romances and friendships are formed, or old ones broken or remade. But for my money, the best and most entertaining stories occur when these things are incidental. In *Mary Poppins*, people get on with things, they 'do' rather than just 'feel', and in the course of the action, feelings are revealed, healed, mended, progressed.

*Mary Poppins* is also a 'rite of passage' story in the way that it shows us the children growing up and learning to see their own parents as fallible humans, while they develop a more mature understanding of how they fit into the world. But really it is a good 'hero's journey' story – according to the criteria defined by Joseph Campbell back in 1949.

This type of story begins in the 'ordinary world', where we establish what is 'normal life' for the hero but then at some point they encounter a threat, which may be tangible or existential, but it undermines what they felt sure of. They realise they must act but are too scared or inexperienced to do it alone. So they meet their mentor – someone who will guide them through it all. The hero then goes through a series of tests and threats, meeting allies and enemies, before the climax of a huge ordeal that shows them what they're really made of. All this takes place in a world that is unfamiliar or daunting for them but still they must prevail. Then, having won, they must return to their ordinary world safely and bring home the message – the reward – of what they have learned and in so doing, they save not only themselves but everyone else too.

If you're thinking that I have gone back into some obscure corner of literary theory, it's worth bearing in mind that many of the top-grossing films of all time fall into this category (*Star Wars* being the most notorious example) and it is a template known, loved and utilised by some of the most successful people in film. So it's an interesting study to make, especially if you would like to write the script of a movie that makes millions worldwide. But when we examine the structure of *Mary Poppins*, something rather unexpected emerges, as to who exactly the hero is.

I think it is reasonable and likely that many people will immediately think of Mary Poppins as the story's hero – I certainly did. It makes sense in some respects and she is the title character after all. But as you map the journey, you start to wonder. Perhaps Mr Banks is the hero? His journey also has elements of the hero's journey structure. However, as you go on, you find something quite exciting: in fact, the characters whose journeys most map onto the structure are none other than the children, Jane and Michael. They are the heroes, they undertake the journey, they face the danger, beat the enemy and return home to save everyone in their family and, most importantly, their father.

*Mary Poppins* is a hero's journey story about a pair of children saving their father. They need to save a man who they love, who is danger of ending his life 'having never done a single thing' he really wanted to – his restoration to the heart of their family is the reward they bring home. It seems inconceivable to me that a storyteller as experienced as Disney was unaware of the work of Joseph Campbell. He also shared Travers' deep need to address his childhood relationship with a father figure.

So, it really is 'saving Mr Banks'. It really is what Travers always wanted, and Disney made it happen. She must have felt quite exposed, somehow, and vulnerable and, from what I have read about her, I think she might have found that a very uncomfortable experience. For that, I am sorry for her. But the work is sublime.

I think this may be why P L Travers had such a strong reaction viewing *Mary Poppins* for the first time. Tears gleamed in her eyes as she sat in the crowded movie theatre on the night of the premiere. And though she hated the animation with every fibre of her being and found the sugary sentiment (as she saw it) unforgivable, perhaps as an avid and learned student of narrative and myth, she couldn't help but see that the skill and precision of some of the world's finest storytellers, in the form of Disney and his writers, musicians and animators, had somehow crystallised everything that had been raging inside her since she was a girl.

The books, though they are wonderful, don't do anything like this – they are rangy and imprecise. But sometimes it takes the laser focus, the running-time limitation of a film, to make the story at the heart of any successful creative endeavour – the real story, the very deepest and most profound story – take flight, and soar. When you get a story right, it will last forever. It is both human and divine. And that is *Mary Poppins*.

Disney found a way to make *Mary Poppins* moving and coherent and uncover a deeper truth. And though Travers may have resented the product of his endeavours, she must have respected his skill on some level because at one point she even wanted to make a sequel, though Disney had died in 1966. In the mid-1980s, she even wrote a script called 'Mary Poppins Comes Back' with friend, collaborator and respected writer Brian Sibley, but it wasn't the right time and, twenty years after the first film, casting was a particular issue.

Some believe Travers hated the film for the rest of her life, but in an interview with the BBC in 2013 (ahead of the release of the actual sequel starring Emily Blunt, *Mary Poppins Returns*), Sibley describes watching *Mary Poppins* with Travers, and says she had mellowed significantly by then. He explained:

> 'Throughout the film she gave me notes. There were one or two moments where she said, "Oh that's terrible." But there were more where she got excited at what was up there on screen. She patted my hand and said, "Oh we must remember that, that's excellent, I like that bit very much ..."'

I would love to know what those bits are! But I'm glad Travers made her peace with it to some extent in the end. She never saw the sequel to *Mary Poppins* that was eventually made of course, as she died in 1996, but the truth and joy of the story she helped to create lives on and on.

# Chapter 9

# Step In Time

In 2014, I wrote a novel called *Brenda Monk is Funny*. It was about a young woman called Brenda Monk (no points for working that out) who becomes a stand-up comedian. It charts her first year in comedy from her first ever gig to her own show at the Edinburgh Festival twelve months later. She is in her twenties and in a seriously toxic relationship with a more successful stand-up, who uses her and their dysfunctional romance for material. She dumps him, sleeps around a bit, finds a new boyfriend, swears a lot, takes some drugs, drinks too much and generally behaves very much as a stand-up comedian in her twenties would. Accusations that it is very 'autobiographical' are (ahem) unfounded . . .

I was very proud of it, though, and I still am. I think it's one of the best things I have written. And one of the most wonderful things about the whole experience was how creatively free it was, especially compared to working in TV and film, where you can expect endless notes from around fifteen people in the food chain before you get anywhere near a cast or a camera. Everyone has an opinion and the writer can often get sidelined. But in the world of publishing it is quite different. The writer is the sole creator and the purity of their vision is guarded by all with a tenacity that makes you want to cry. It is quite amazing.

Around six months after the book was published, I happened to be sat next to a very senior comedy commissioner at a party. We made some industry small talk and, as is normal in these circumstances, she asked me what I had been up to lately. So I told her all about my book. I had barely finished explaining the basic premise before she jumped in and interrupted me.

'Ooh, actually that sounds really interesting – how old is Brenda?'

'Twenty-nine,' I said.

She screwed up her face. 'No, you see that wouldn't work for us. How about this – Brenda is a 42-year-old married mum of two, who works in a supermarket at the checkout by day and secretly becomes a comedian by night. Her husband doesn't know, it's a secret, and she has to carry on as normal, making him his tea and looking after her kids and holding down her job and then gigging at night. We would be looking for a pre-watershed slot, so it would have to be clean – no sex or swearing and also I think it would be great if she had some sort of cancer, maybe breast cancer – our female audience really responds to characters who have breast cancer.'

This is not a lie. This actually happened. I sat silently for a minute and then said quietly, 'OK, but I mean, that's really nothing to do with my book.'

She nodded, half listening. 'Yeah, but we'd only really need the title. You could definitely pitch to write on it.'

'Thanks,' I whispered, and she smiled and turned to the person on her left.

Needless to say, I never heard another thing about it. Such is the world of television. And it's not that her idea was terrible, it just had nothing to do with my idea, *my* book, my actual book that I had written, and she didn't care. She didn't even let me explain the idea or the story. She just trampled all over it, with a fairly unoriginal take and an eye on the advertising revenue for a certain demographic. But I don't expect anything else – I've worked in TV for twenty years and this is usually how it goes.

So, when I read for the first time of P L Travers' reluctance to sell Walt Disney her *Mary Poppins* books to make into a film, I understood her caution. These days, when I write something original I have a better understanding of what I would be dealing with in the event that someone bought the option to make it on screen and I brace myself accordingly and have better contracts to protect myself, so I am more prepared. And of course, the money earned from a successful project is nice. But Travers was not an experienced film writer, she knew little of the medium. Why should she give Disney her life's work, even for a generous sum? She believed she would lose control of her creation.

Disney pursued her for two decades. Travers' biographer describes him as a 'master of persistence'. During this period, he was building a company of remarkable imagination, creativity and technical prowess. There was no one like him. He was a contentious figure, not always popular, and known for a ruthlessness that could wind a person. Sometimes his creations were unsuccessful, commercially and critically. His judgement regarding representation and diversity was not always sound, as *Song of the South*, his 1946 film featuring the rightly discredited 'happy slave' trope, showed. But his energy and commitment still made him the leader in his field. Nothing stopped him from creating and innovating. He was relentless.

Disney created Mickey Mouse in 1928 and the cartoons he voiced himself quickly went from being an instant hit to an iconic image familiar around the world (put three black circles over each other, one big, two small and almost anyone will recognise it instantly). Disney introduced three-colour glass plate technology to create those gorgeous backdrops that seem to go on and on and was also the first to produce feature-length animated films with synchronised sound (where the audio recording properly matches the visuals). *Snow White* (1937), *Dumbo* (1941) and *Bambi* (1942) showed an ambition for animation that nobody had ever considered before. He built a huge independent studio in Burbank that could rival any of the greats such as MGM. He changed the entire industry on his own.

By the early 1950s, Walt Disney's two young daughters had already been badgering him about making a *Mary Poppins* film for years. They were fans of the books and through them he had come to love them too. He found Poppins an intriguing proposition and he was hungry for new family stories to tell. He liked the idea of a mysterious nanny coming into a dysfunctional home and making things better. For him, it had a personal element. He had endured a miserable childhood at the hands of his repressive, cruel and financially mean father, Elias, who used corporal punishment liberally and didn't allow his children any toys to play with. Walt grew up on a farm and had a punishing round of chores. It is thought that his relationship with the animals on the farm and in the surrounding area, in the absence of anything else that was joyful or kind, may have contributed to his love of bringing them to life through his animation.

In the summer of 1910, when Walt was nine, Disney Sr moved his family to Kansas City and the real misery years began. As Elias failed at venture after venture, becoming increasingly violent and difficult, Walt and his brother Roy went to work to help the family keep things together. They would rise at 3.30am to undertake multiple newspaper delivery routes, then find other income anywhere they could whilst also doing their chores. Walt discovered his love of drawing around this age and later found he could sell his pictures around town.

It may be a coincidence that Disney's *Mary Poppins* is set in 1910, unlike the books, but it doesn't strike me that much happened by coincidence in Walt's tightly controlled, micro-managed career. It seems to me that, on some level, he wanted Mary Poppins to have entered his childhood at exactly the same time she enters Jane and Michael's. Perhaps she could save them all.

Travers finally agreed to sell the rights to Disney in 1959, the excitement of which was enough to bring Walt back to the studio. He had been absent throughout much of the 1950s, his mind on other projects. He had put key animators in charge of his various productions and had somewhat eccentrically occupied himself by building his extra-large toy train set (he could sit on the engine as it went around the tracks), whilst he planned and oversaw the construction of Disneyland, which opened in Anaheim, California in 1955. The arrival of a signed contract saying he could make *Mary Poppins* at long last brought him back to his first love – movie making.

Julie Andrews was cast in the role of Mary Poppins on the strength of her Broadway success in several roles, including Eliza Doolittle in *My Fair Lady* (the film part went to Audrey Hepburn in the same year as *Mary Poppins* was begun). She was pregnant when Disney offered her the part but he wanted her to play Poppins so much that he agreed to defer filming for a year – despite the fact that this was her first ever Hollywood film.

The rest of the casting was a crucial as the title role. Dick Van Dyke came on board to play Bert. By this stage, he was a very well-known entertainer in the United States, via his CBS TV programme, *The Dick Van Dyke Show*. *Mary Poppins* was his breakout film role, achieving a level of success in the film world that he struggled to match in his later career, though he remains a huge star thanks to his TV work. Bert is still the part he is probably most famous for, other than playing himself, but deservedly so.

Disney cast English actors David Tomlinson as George Banks and Glynis Johns as his wife Winifred. Tomlinson was a relatively well-established actor at this point and, though he felt he was becoming typecast in roles he described as 'normal professional idiot', he played them with such deftness that he remained much in demand for these parts. Disney seemed to enjoy his performance as George Banks as he went on to cast him in *Bedknobs and Broomsticks* and he was named as a Disney Legend and inducted into the Disney Hall of Fame in 2000. However, apparently (according to a piece by Giulia Rhodes in the *Telegraph*, December 2018) he was not impressed when he first saw a rough cut of *Mary Poppins* – he was 'convinced it would flop. He thought it was sentimental rubbish'.

Glynis Johns was probably the most experienced film actor in *Mary Poppins* at the time of filming. She was the veteran of dozens of movies by 1964 and had worked with major stars such as Richard Todd, David Niven and Danny Kaye. She was also a famed Broadway star, and the beautiful and haunting 'Send in the Clowns' was written for her by Stephen Sondheim for his musical *A Little Night Music*. Knowing her power, Johns was only willing to take the part of Mrs

Banks if she had a decent scene and song and so 'Sister Suffragette' was written specifically with the purpose of convincing her. And it did. Of course it did – it's an absolute cracker and it starts the whole thing off on the right track. She obviously knew what she was worth and she was right – after all, in convincing both Sondheim and the Sherman Brothers to write bespoke pieces for her to perform, she effectively had three of the greatest songwriters of the twentieth century eating out of her hand. *Mary Poppins* really wouldn't be the same film without her – it takes some charm, some twinkle, to make Mrs Banks negligent but likeable.

Katie Nanna was played by Elsa Lanchester and, though her appearance is brief, it is also memorable, and worth noting. By the time *Mary Poppins* came along, Lanchester was a woman with quite a career behind her. She had studied dance in Paris as young woman, taught by Isadora Duncan. She went on to appear in cabaret in London, and ran her own night club, The Cave of Harmony, in Seven Dials, London, in the late 1920s. She famously played the Bride of Frankenstein in the film of the same name in 1935. No wonder she makes such an impression.

Ed Wynn took on the role of Uncle Albert. He was an actor and comedian who had already won a Peabody Award and worked with Buster Keaton and Lucille Ball, and he knew exactly what to do with Albert because of his long experience in physical comedy. Reginald Owen, known for playing Scrooge in the 1938 film of *A Christmas Carol*, became Admiral Boom, and so the stage was set. Disney could not have hoped for a better cast of stellar cameos.

Julie Andrews talks of the experience of making the film in her autobiography, *Home Work*. The dance training was gruelling but she was used to a formidable rehearsal schedule from her West End and Broadway days. What she was amazed by was the speed of the filming itself and the lack of actual acting rehearsal and direction. She was unnerved by the fact that in each scene she might only get a few goes at it before the director was happy with the take and they would move on. She didn't feel she knew enough about herself as a performer to be able to sense whether she had given a satisfactory version or if she would be happy with it when she saw it.

Remember Andrews had seen very little of herself on film before and it is notoriously difficult to get right, especially for theatre actors used to giving bigger performances that reach to the back of an auditorium. It was famously exemplified by Richard Burton and Elizabeth Taylor – Burton was a celebrated stage actor; Taylor was a movie star. The first time they worked together on the film *Cleopatra*, Burton recalls not understanding her style at first, saying, 'It looked like she was doing nothing, but then when I saw it on screen I realised she was doing everything.' He was not the first great actor to be flummoxed by the intimacy and subtlety of film acting – Laurence Olivier before him had had a similar experience with Marilyn Monroe in *The Prince and the Showgirl*, where he found himself envious of her natural ability to communicate with the camera in a way that, even with all his training and acclaim, he could never quite achieve.

But, like Taylor and Monroe, Julie Andrews clearly had a natural feel for it and somehow, by instinct and good casting, she makes Mary Poppins everything you want her to be. I asked Karen Dotrice, who played Jane Banks, how she felt about filming with Andrews and she told me:

*'As Jane/Karen, I felt very much like her daughter and that she really loved me. We shot the scene 'Stay Awake' after a long day of filming and the lights were hot. I was snuggled under my satin comforter and Julie's voice and touch of her hand put me flat out. Fasto, they had to keep waking me up to reshoot! She had that calming, loving feeling and I trusted her completely. At that young age and on a long shoot, it all seems like real life. So she mummied me a lot. When she had the electronic robin on her arm in "Spoonful of Sugar" she knew I was fascinated by how it worked under her sleeve, and we'd sit in-between takes and she'd let me explore the wiring and robotics. For me, Mary Poppins was, and probably is real.'*

Julie Andrews' portrayal was certainly everything Disney wanted Poppins to be. However, Pamela Travers felt differently. Though she was not directly rude or critical of Andrews, she was not pleased with how pretty Andrews was, nor how kind. The original Poppins was meant to be 'plain' and quite brusque and short with the children. She felt there was too much sugar on the spoon here. Though this didn't stop Travers and Andrews becoming pen pals – Andrews had sensed the tension between Travers and Disney and had undertaken to write with updates to Travers, who was in London for the duration of the filming, so she wouldn't feel entirely shut out.

I asked Emma Thompson, who is, among her other talents, an Oscar winning screen-writer what she thought about the battle between Travers and Disney. She said:

*'I totally sympathised with her struggle to de-sweeten and de-whimsify the Disney version. She was a superb writer and her*

*books repay visiting again and again – the first Mary Poppins is an extraordinary book and the character entirely different to that one portrayed so beautifully and kindly by Julie. But Poppins was no spoonful of sugar. She was sharp and fast and funny and original and not pretty, I don't think. So I totally understood Pamela's desperate need to protect her creation from what she saw – and I cannot help but partially agree – as bastardisation. The way in which she conducted her battles was unfeeling though – she had very little sense of humour when it came down to it and she was deeply contemptuous of the young men trying to write the music. She treated them very badly and for that there is no excuse, actually.'*

Ah yes, the songs. They really are sublime. Long-time Disney collaborators, brothers Richard M Sherman and Robert B Sherman, excelled themselves with their music and lyrics, while the score was arranged and conducted by Irwin Kostal. By the time the film was out and the awards season over, all three had received dozens of nominations and won a Grammy and an Oscar for Best Song for 'Chim Chim Cher-ee', a beguiling melody about the luck chimney sweeps bring, written in a minor key which gives it a strangely melancholy air, despite its playful, upbeat lyrics.

They also cleverly drew on Edwardian music hall motifs to give the music a traditional flavour that felt authentic and nostalgic. This suited Julie Andrews well as she had started out as a young girl in the music halls and vaudeville shows of London. She recalled finding her solo in 'Supercalifragilisticexpialidocious' especially enjoyable and familiar as it was reminiscent of the fast patter songs she had performed to great applause many years earlier.

But this was no pastiche. On viewing *Mary Poppins* in 2020, the songs are still as astonishingly light and catchy, the lyrics as deft and witty and moving where required as they felt in 1964. There isn't a dud in it. This is likely due to the huge number of pieces that were written and then cut – in fact, a further thirteen songs were written and not used and another eight themes or melodic lines were created but later deployed to other Disney films such as *Bedknobs and Broomsticks* and *The Jungle Book*. To say it was an embarrassment of riches would be an understatement.

The talent of the Sherman brothers actually leaves me almost tearful – such immense feeling, skill and humanity is moving. It was their father, Al Sherman, also a songwriter, who dared them to write some songs together when they were in their early twenties. His encouragement led to the most successful partnership in film music ever known – in fact, the Sherman brothers wrote more film scores than any other writer in history and are the most garlanded.

Travers wasn't so keen. She didn't quite get it. In an article for the *New York Times* by Margy Rochlin, the then 85-year-old Richard Sherman recalled his experience: 'She didn't care about our feelings, how she chopped us apart,' he said with a shudder. Travers wasn't just sharp-tongued, he added, she also misunderstood the meaning of original score. Often, after they'd finish singing her a song, she would scoff at their labours and then suggest replacements, such as vaudeville classics. 'She said, "I rather fancy 'Ta-ra-ra Boom-de-ay',"' said Mr Sherman, still able to summon up his exasperation with the author.

In his recollection, Disney loathed negativity. 'He'd kill you if you said you didn't like something,' Mr. Sherman said, explaining how dissenters were dealt with in what he described as group punch-up sessions with various departments. 'He'd say, "If you can't think of something to improve it, then keep your mouth shut."'

So how did Disney deal with the unremitting invective levelled at the Shermans by Travers? 'He'd say to us: "Keep going. Don't let her get to you." He didn't sit in the room with us listening to the insults, but he knew what they were.'

This bears out Emma Thompson's observation that even with the most sympathetic interpretation of Pamela Travers' discomfort with the film of *Mary Poppins*, her behaviour towards the Sherman brothers was inexcusable. She should have known she was in the presence of greatness. But perhaps she did and that was part of the problem. Music can touch depths that other creative forms of expression can't. As the comedian Sara Pascoe says, 'I don't like music. I don't want to have an emotion I didn't have a minute ago, thank you.' She's joking, of course, but perhaps not entirely.

It seems to me that Pamela Travers was all about control, and that extended to her own emotions. For someone unused to having long-buried feelings push their way up, particularly in front of other people, it must have been terrifying to have the long fingers of those melodies and lyrics reach inside her and yank up an emotion that she would rather had stayed where it was. To be moved to tears by music, in public, is something only those who are totally at ease with themselves and their feelings can tolerate. I know I struggle with it. I feel a little for her here – perhaps she used rudeness as a defence, a way to keep herself under control. She wouldn't be the first.

But luckily Walt Disney knew he had something extraordinary on his hands. When he wanted to close a deal, or raise more funding for a project, he would get the potential investors in a room with a piano and the Sherman brothers and just let them work their magic. It almost never failed. 'Feed the Birds' was a particular favourite of Disney's, as Robert Sherman recalled:

> *'On Fridays, after work, Walt would often invite us into his office and we'd talk about things that were going on at the studio. After a while, he'd wander to the north window, look out into the distance and just say, "Play it." And Dick [Richard Sherman] would wander over to the piano and play "Feed the Birds" for him. One time, just as Dick was almost finished, under his breath, I heard Walt say, "Yep. That's what it's all about."'*

Predictably Travers didn't like it; hilariously she wanted 'Greensleeves' instead – that fey classic attributed to Henry VIII and now most often heard via the chimes of an ice-cream van – but Disney wasn't letting her have her way. Sherman has also observed that 'Feed the Birds' is one of the few commercial songs about the merits of charitable giving, and this also seemed to strike a chord with Disney. Sherman later recalled Disney telling him, 'This is the metaphor for the whole film.'

This is one interpretation, but I think there may be more to this 'metaphor' idea for Disney. I think it's not about capitalism, or charity, but rather about making small gestures that mean a lot to somebody else. To be generous with the things we have to give, no matter how humble. Having had a hard and cruel father himself, Disney would have been alive to this message that we can so easily please our children by giving the smallest, simplest things in a way that perhaps the more loved Shermans weren't. In fact, you could argue that Disney's whole career, his entire raison d'etre, was to be found in providing a safe environment for children to grow up in, to be carefree and happy in, even if just for a few hours. And also to teach adults to be children again. It's certainly what *Mary Poppins* does.

With the casting taken care of, the songs in place and Travers if not on board then at least relatively under control, the filming continued smoothly. Dick Van Dyke brought every bit of his long and wide-ranging experience to the role of Bert, though famously he was not able to conquer the cockney accent – it is truly terrible, and so much remarked upon so there is little to add here. Suffice to say, it stands alone as one of the worst British accents ever committed to film, and he knows it.

However, Van Dyke did offer a hilarious and self-deprecating apology for it in 2017 when he was chosen by BAFTA as the recipient of the Britannia Award for excellence in television. In response, he said, 'I appreciate this opportunity to apologise to the members of BAFTA for inflicting on them the most atrocious cockney accent in the history of cinema.'

One thing Van Dyke did thoroughly conquer was playing the additional part of Mr Dawes Sr – whose fusty RP British accent is far more convincing. He desperately wanted to do it, but Disney didn't believe he could pull it off convincingly. In the end, Walt agreed so long as Van Dyke was willing to do it for free – he was not paid any additional fee for the increase in work (and time in the make-up chair).

In the end, it was worse than that (or better, if you happened to be Walt) because in a *20/20 Special* about *Mary Poppins*, aired in the USA in 2018, Van Dyke revealed to *Hamilton* composer Lin-Manuel Miranda, 'I had to go to Walt and ask him for the part. He wouldn't give it to me. I said, "I'll do it for nothing." Actually, I had to give him $4,000 – I paid *him* to do the part . . . and I'd do it again.'

Dick Van Dyke was no idiot – by the time the script of *Mary Poppins* came along in 1963, containing the part of Bert, he knew this was going to be something special. He was already a huge star and nobody reaches the level of fame and success he had achieved without being able to sniff out a winner. No wonder he was so keen to be in it as much as he could. In fact, he also told Miranda in the same interview that when he heard the news of a sequel, he said, 'Well, I got excited, of course. My first question was, "Can I be in it?"' (Which he was, at the age of 91, playing Dawes Jr this time, dancing on a desk.)

The main filming took place over nine months, and then there was a further eight months of post-production animation work to complete. Not all the stunts were animated, some had been made for real. In an interview for the website Culturewhisper.com, Karen Dotrice remembered, 'In the tea party scene we were suspended from wires above the ground with mattresses on the floor in case we fell. Us kids probably would have been fine if we'd fallen but for Ed Wynn [who played Uncle Albert] it would have been a bit sketchy.' Once the scene was successfully completed without incident, the wires had to be meticulously painted out by hand in post-production.

Dotrice went on to explain how the 'Jolly Holiday' sequence took at least a week to film and was a new experience for her technically: 'Remember, we were looking at cartoons that hadn't been drawn, so what we were actually looking at were rather sweaty, middle-aged men carrying cardboard cut-outs of donkeys or penguins, dancing around in front of us for eye-lines. Dick was always making terribly funny comments and cracking us up. So no wonder it took so long to film!'

But with the live action shooting finally done, the animation could get underway, and of course this was where the unique magic of Disney came in. Walt wanted to oversee everything, just as he had when he began his company. He didn't know it, but this would be the last fully realised feature film he worked on before he died. He gave it everything, and accounts from those who worked with him at this time record that he appeared happy, whereas in the past he could be autocratic and moody. It seemed this whole project delighted Disney, and that love and excitement translates itself to the screen.

*Mary Poppins* was released on 27 August 1964, to almost immediate critical acclaim. The premiere, held at Grauman's Chinese Theatre in Los Angeles, was a huge affair. Pamela L Travers had not been invited officially, though she had managed to get a ticket from an unsuspecting Disney executive and took her place inside to finally see, after months of post-production, the fruits of all their labour. She wasn't especially happy. She had words with Walt Disney at the party afterwards, was firmly rebuffed and went back to London. She never spoke to anyone involved in the making of *Mary Poppins* again.

It's sad that Travers could not participate in the success of *Mary*

*Poppins* but you have to respect her for keeping her own boundaries, just as rigorously as her own creation would. Despite her creative quarrel, she certainly enjoyed new riches, which made her financially comfortable and then some for the rest of her life. So there was some reward at least and she continued to write further Mary Poppins books that enjoyed far more interest as a result of the Disney film. She died in 1996, wealthy, and as great a mystery as ever she was.

Meanwhile, *Mary Poppins* the movie was an unstoppable juggernaut. It had been a long time coming but perhaps was all the sweeter for it. It was almost universally well reviewed – the *Hollywood Reporter* said it was 'a triumph'; the *New York Times* said it was a 'wonderful, cheering movie'. Audiences agreed and, from a budget of around $5 million, the box office return from the initial cinema release was $31 million, making it one of the most profitable films of the year 1964/65. With the chunk of money *Mary Poppins* brought Disney, he was able to buy a large amount of land in Orlando, Florida, on which he built Disney World, the natural step up from Disneyland in California. He installed a mono-rail system to carry people around the park and, in tribute to his best performing film for nearly two decades, he named the safety system on the railway MaPo (after Mary Poppins). She was even looking after people via the feat of engineering now.

*Mary Poppins* was nominated for Best Picture at the 1965 Oscars, though it did not win – *My Fair Lady* did. But, in a neat reversal, Julie Andrews beat Audrey Hepburn (as Eliza Doolittle) to the Best Actress Oscar. *My Fair Lady* was also made in 1964 and set in Edwardian London. It was Julie Andrews who had made the role famous on Broadway, but she had been passed over by the film producers for Hepburn who was a bigger star, though she couldn't sing (all her vocal performances were dubbed by Marni Nixon). It doesn't sound like Andrews was too bitter though and she certainly had no need to be when she won the Oscar for *Mary Poppins*. She also won the Golden Globe that year and couldn't resist having a little dig in her acceptance speech, thanking the producer of *My Fair Lady*, Jack L Warner (of Warner Bros) for not casting her . . . ! See? Andrews isn't always as sweet as she looks, and all the better for it.

The two films remain intertwined for many reasons and they have danced a jig around each other ever since. They seem connected – the themes, the genre, the setting, even the lead actresses – there was something in the air in the early 1960s that meant these two stories of two young women, apparently arising from nowhere, keeping their cool even when all around are losing theirs, hit home with audiences and critics. It was the zeitgeist in the early stirrings of second-wave feminism. They don't tick every box, of course, but there is an edge to both of them that marks a move away from the heroines of the 1950s. Along with Elizabeth Taylor as *Cleopatra*, also released in 1964, independent, single women who take charge of their surroundings seemed to be a trend. It reflected the times, which were changing fast in the 1960s, just as they were in the 1910s. There is a duality to the energy that seems to combine and amplify the message.

*Mary Poppins* is rightly described as Walt Disney's 'crowning achievement'. It remains one of his best-loved films. He died in 1966, two years after it was released. At least he saw one of his most cherished ambitions realised, and with enormous success. It's impossible to know when embarking on a huge project like *Mary Poppins* whether it will be a hit; you need dogged determination, self-belief and indefatigable ambition – all qualities Walt Disney had in spades, and of which Poppins herself would surely approve. If there is a lesson here, it's never give up. If you really want something, you have to keep trying.

# Chapter 10

# Let's Go Fly A Kite

As I was writing this book, the world changed. The virus we all came to know as Covid-19 swept the globe and, as spring burst its buds all around me, it became clear that none of us could predict what the long-term damage would be. I, like many other performers, abruptly lost all my work in that arena overnight. I had never felt so lucky to be writing a book, and I felt pretty lucky already. This examination of Mary Poppins and what she can teach us started as something sincere but playful, but then suddenly became something approaching a necessity for survival. Her practicality and positivity has felt essential for my sanity. It has been sobering, to say the least.

As I sit here at my desk (OK – armchair with an Ikea laptop cushion on my knees and a(nother) doughnut by my side), I can hear my young son playing noisily in the other room, supervised by my ever-patient husband. My step-daughter is in another country, also self-isolating, trying to maintain her education. My parents are in their respective homes, wondering how long the restrictions will last for them.

At least we have the technology to communicate with loved ones who are elsewhere. But in terms of my circumstances, which have shrunk to my immediate surroundings and my immediate family, we are all at home together and already I am grateful for whatever advice I have managed to glean from Mary Poppins as to how to manage myself, my family, and this whole situation with something approaching good grace. I count my blessings daily. I do not whinge – well, not out loud. I eat another doughnut instead (admittedly Poppins might not approve of that). As I am writing this, I actually cannot fly a kite outside for fear of breaking government regulations, and so the kites I fly must be internal. And that's a good lesson too.

When the government's instruction to remain at home was broadcast, I sent a tweet with a bit of advice for staying sane when you have to stay home. I have worked from home for most of my adult life with long periods of writing (or unemployment) punctuated by short, frantic bursts of interaction on film, TV or theatre sets. So, I have at least developed the theory of good practice, even if I have not always followed through. This is what I wrote:

> **@KatyFBrand** Some tips if you are feeling some darkness creeping into you: 1) everyone up, showered and dressed by 9am on weekdays, 2) tidy up and do the dishes before bed – force yourself, 3) change bedding once a week, 4) open all the windows for 10 minutes every morning and evening. X

This has been liked or re-tweeted many thousands of times and, as I think I have established, it's certainly not because I am a domestic genius and it's not because it's especially original advice. It's because when the shit really hits the fan, and when all else fails, some sort of routine is necessary and people will take advice from anyone who can be bothered to offer it. And of course, these are not even really my tips either – they are pure Poppins. I don't really think that I would have written those words if I hadn't been writing this book and therefore immersed in the Poppins Doctrine before the catastrophe started.

My time has been taken from me, condensed, restricted, contained and handed back in a TARDIS-like package that looks small on the outside but, once you stick your head into it, reveals the seconds, minutes, hours, days, weeks, months – maybe even years if the worst is to be believed – stretching out in front of me, whispering with a somewhat mocking tone that I may not have enough stuff to do to fill them. There are only so many times you can disinfect your surfaces in a day before you start to wonder whether you have lost your mind, along with the top layer of skin from your hands. And yes, the spoonful of sugar is very much wrapped around the doughnuts. I hope to god they don't stop me from getting to the doughnuts.

Mary Poppins really has been my spirit guide throughout this strange time. A few days ago, I executed a brutal cull of my young son's toys and now his bedroom is light, fresh and he can actually see what there is to play with. Nothing happened when I snapped my fingers (perhaps I wasn't trying hard enough) but still, there are three bags of broken plastic crap ready to go in the recycling and I feel both better and ashamed for letting it get to this. (And for buying so much plastic crap in the first place.) I had been intending to do this job for months and I hadn't. It has taken a new respect for Mary

Poppins, and a global pandemic, to force me to do it. The former is sweet, the latter not something I wish to repeat, however clean and tidy the house gets.

My underwear drawer is next . . . maybe I will finally have the courage throw away the fifteen pairs of Spanx lurking at the back, clogging up space. I never wear them, because these days I prefer a night out looking a bit lumpy rather than feeling that I am having some sort of lateral abdominal surgery every time I sit down, and then needing a ten-minute rest whenever I attempt to remove them to go to the toilet.

I keep Mary Poppins close now, in my heart. There is something so comforting about her ability to keep herself together, no matter what. P L Travers created her for this purpose and Walt Disney may have added a layer of sentiment, but he maintained her sense of stoicism. Though sharing our feelings with the right people is undoubtedly important, I don't want to live in a world where emotion is the only currency. I don't want to be needy or indulge my every whim. It leads to sluggishness, a clogging of both the arteries and the synapses.

It's good to talk, and that has been the trend of the twenty-first century, but it's also good to shut up sometimes. It's right to be able to express our emotions and ask for help, but it's also right to know when we are capable of helping ourselves. Through an explosion in reality TV and a sort of pseudo-therapy layer of amateur counsellors, who offer endless and exhausting advice on how to be happy all the time, we have ended up feeding our neuroses and wondering why we are no more content than we were before. If anything, we are less happy. So, it's good to share, but you don't have to share everything all the time with a global audience of strangers. There is nothing wrong with telling a few people, taking some advice and then getting over it, if that's all it needs. Some stoicism is not a sign of mental ill health. Sometimes it can be the opposite.

Mary Poppins is the icon we need to redress the balance. We can have secrets. We can have privacy. We can have boundaries. But the real message of *Mary Poppins* is that it is in our power to be happy or not, that we have the tools immediately at hand to at least be happier than we are now. Having a good tidy-up, for a start, is often the most basic advice a mental health expert will give anyone who is struggling. Go outside. Try to see a friend. Ask for help. Bert and Mary get it – two people who between them seem to own a box of chalk, a chimney brush and a carpet bag of random stuff. And a one-man band kit, admittedly, but you do have to put that down at some point – it's not as portable as it looks.

And yet it's so easy to become George Banks, obsessed with status and security, finance and filial piety, that we miss what's important. Or Winifred Banks, so caught up in her own world of campaigning that she loses any sense of perspective, happy to dump her kids wherever she can, always rushing out to somewhere more exciting, leaving her responsibilities to any passing stranger (luckily Bert, in this case . . . ). Of course, these characters are extreme and funny, though they still have something to admire at their core. No one should forget about work or having a life outside of being a parent, but this is a reminder that if more homely concerns slide completely out of view, we will not necessarily be the happier for it.

The biggest revelation for me in writing this, and looking at *Mary Poppins* more closely, was that the children are the heroes of the story. Believing Mary Poppins is the hero is an easy mistake to make but once you have identified the true nature of the story in the film, on the deepest structural level, it becomes clear that Jane and Michael are the heroes. It is touching beyond belief to find that what most of us are responding to, the reason the film has lasted so long and is such a firm favourite to this day and feels as fresh as ever, is that we want to save our parents. And that when we become parents ourselves, of course we want to love our children and be their protectors, but that we also want to be educated by them. Maybe even saved by them.

So many people I know talk about being a 'mess' before they had kids, at which point they were forced to grow up. I can certainly relate to that, as I have detailed throughout this book. But the awful truth is that we don't really sort ourselves out when we have children, it's just that the pace of life increases rapidly and responsibilities fly into your face continually and unceasingly. The minute-by-minute needs, the shout of 'MUMMY!' every four minutes, the inability to even go to the toilet alone or eat a bag of crisps without giving 90 per cent of them away mean that we push down anything that does not require immediate attention. You don't start trying to solve your own relationship with food, for example, or money, or anything, while driving in a blizzard. You just deal with what's in front of your face and this goes on for about eighteen years, if you're lucky, by which point you're so knackered and broken that all you want to do is be left alone to whatever vices you have managed to preserve.

But *Mary Poppins* tells us it doesn't have to be like this. It doesn't have to be a battleground. You can view your children as comrades, rather than subjects. And though Mary Poppins is firm and has boundaries and will not give up her privacy, her dignity or her days off, she is also surprisingly liberal and easy-going. She never patronises the children and, despite singing about spoonfuls of the stuff, she doesn't sugar-coat anything either. She is actually quite brutal with them from time to time, telling it like it is. I find this as comforting as anything else because, whilst of course you do not want to frighten or traumatise your children, Mary Poppins shows you can share more than you think. And often there's no point in pretending anyway. Children always know when there's tension around and it's easier for them to handle if they have a sense of what's going on. It makes them more resilient. Bert knows this too – he gives Jane and Michael an honest window into what it's like to be George Banks and this leads them to help their father in a way they could never have anticipated at the start of the story.

So, yes there are the obvious things we can do – I can do – to be a better parent, such as tidy up properly and often, keep order in the house, look after myself and my appearance, maintain strict bedtimes, sing with robins as the opportunity arises and so on. But the more subtle message is 'be a family together', keep your children close, learn from them even as you teach them and let them teach you, too. Children are very good at reminding you of what's important. Almost as good as reminding you that your tummy has got noticeably bigger because you have been eating too many crisps. They will poke it. They will do this and they will do it in front of guests, even as you are eating said crisps.

The lessons to be learned from *Mary Poppins* about being a woman and being a man are also touching and powerful. Nobody is a straightforward representation of their gender and that's a good thing, especially in this time where the notion of gender is under review. The ways in which we are taught to conform over a lifetime both explicitly and implicitly are gently mocked, then challenged, then overturned throughout the film. You can be a mother, and a wife, but maybe somebody else looks after your children, maybe you go out campaigning for something you believe in, maybe you don't really cook a single thing anyone eats in the house (we all have 'Cook' now – it's called an M&S ready meal for four). This does not mean you should be punished. Maybe your kids will be fine, maybe your family will still flourish. Being present is not the same as being a slave. You can be engaged without losing every single thing about yourself.

Absent mothers are often punished in films – their children will be taken to hospital, or go off the rails, or shout abuse at them. It's to *Mary Poppins'* eternal credit that Winifred Banks is pretty outrageous throughout and all she gets at the end is a lovely kite festival and two loving, happy children. Why shouldn't this be the story for her? Why shouldn't we rip up some of the rules that say any mother who is not a sacrificial lamb to her offspring is not worthy of a happy ending? This is some serious feminism, created in the early days of mainstream feminism itself (1963) and set in a time (1910) when it was just a mere twinkle in Glynis Johns' very twinkly eyes.

And of course, George Banks learns how to be a father by losing everything he thinks it takes to be a man. He loses the respect of his domestic staff, the obedience of his wife, the worship of his children and he loses his job. And in the end, he is all the better for it. The strain of keeping it all together breaks; he can look at a man like Bert – someone he would previously have barely acknowledged as he passed him in the street – and see that he holds all the riches of the world.

There is an old story about a man who runs a book shop with books stacked high all around him in precarious piles that reach to the ceiling. The man is known for being a nervous wreck all the time, terrified that at any moment it will all collapse. He lives for years in a state of high anxiety, unable to enjoy anything, unable to relax. One day, a child comes into the shop and, eagerly pulling a picture book from the bottom of a pile, the worst happens and everything comes tumbling to the ground. And, to the amazement of all who know the man, instead of clutching at his heart or dropping to the ground, a huge smile suddenly breaks across his face, his shoulders drop and he falls among the ruins of his shop laughing like he never has before. Finally, finally, the worst thing he could imagine happening has happened and the relief is immense. He can stop worrying about it. He is delighted – a changed man – and he lives happy ever after.

And so it is with George Banks – his story mirrors this old tale almost exactly, even down to the hysterical laughter he is engulfed with at the bank as he is being stripped of his dignity and his career. He laughs. He can't stop. He is finally free. His worst nightmare has occurred and suddenly he sees he will survive it after all. Not just survive but thrive. He is suddenly reconnected with what is important, which has been hidden behind the edifice of his pride all these years, and he skips home to mend his son's kite, free at last.

Ideally, one would achieve this sort of freedom without having your worst nightmare materialise before your very eyes, but it depends how deep into your delusion you have sunk. I have, over the course of my life, had several worst-case scenarios develop financially, professionally and personally, and sometimes the worst has come to pass. I have survived them all thus far and sometimes I have even been able to steady myself before the moment of true reckoning by giving myself up to my certain, or perhaps uncertain, fate: relax into it, let it unfold, try to learn something. It feels good to just give in sometimes, to say there is nothing more I can do, to accept the humiliation and find your dignity within it, even if it's deferred.

I can relate to George Banks as much as anyone – to release your grip on something that is too heavy to hold any more and watch it fall away, and then straighten your fingers, waggle them a bit and walk off constitutes the actions of a free person. I don't always manage it, but I feel lighter when I do.

And as for Mary Poppins herself, I still feel a quickening of excitement in my stomach whenever I think of her. She is a thrilling proposition – a woman so wholly without needs, without shame, without burden. She knows herself. She knows her talents, but also her limits. She has strictly enforced personal boundaries and doesn't care if you don't like her because of them. She shares not one thing more than she wants to. She will not explain herself and sees no reason why she should. She is fearless. She is replete. She is beautifully turned out, dignified and calm. She is a witch. She is mysterious. She is simply herself and she thinks that is enough. She is also cocky, vain, self-regarding, infuriating and stubborn. She gaslights the Banks family something rotten, she leads Bert on, she takes no responsibility for anything she does and then she leaves the moment she's had enough. I love her.

The year 2020 has been terribly hard for everyone, everywhere. Our response to the virus that has ripped round the world, taking so many with it, shutting down our jobs, our lives, separating us from our families and bringing a level of fear and anxiety about everything from how we make and distribute money, to the very things that underpin our civilisation, has required a level of stoicism that most of us were not prepared for.

As I write, I still don't know how or when it will end. I am glad to have had Mary Poppins with me, though. Her fortitude, her practicality and her attitude have been an inspiration. But here's the most encouraging thing – she is Practically Perfect. She is not Absolutely Perfect or Completely Perfect, but Practically Perfect.

This leaves a little room for failure, for slippage. 'Practically' means almost entirely, but not quite. We can make mistakes. We can still be loved and understood even when the world we know is crumbling around us. We cannot choose the era we live in, but we can choose to make the best of whatever we've got and be a bit more Poppins in the smallest of ways. We can appreciate the 'miracle of the everyday'. We can put our best foot forward. We can take our medicine with a spoonful of sugar. We'll find the magic where we can along the way. Onward, then. Well begun is half done. Spit-spot.

# Acknowledgements

*F*irst thanks go to Lisa Milton, publisher at HQ, and my agent Cathryn Summerhayes at Curtis Brown Group. Thank you both for being so supportive, encouraging and swift! It makes a huge difference to know two such experienced and extraordinarily talented women are with me.

Thanks to Kate Fox and Liz Marvin for editing the book and giving notes that helped me organise, improve and focus what I was trying to say. The distance between this book and the first draft is so immense it makes me wince and that is your doing (in a good way...)

Thanks to Jess Molloy and Sile Edwards at Curtis Brown for always smoothing the path with patience and grace.

Thanks to Sophie Calder, Lily Capewell and all at HQ who are in the business of producing, promoting and marketing this book. Without you, no one would know about it!

Thanks to Emma Thompson, Victoria Coren Mitchell, Karen Dotrice, Michele Dotrice, Andrew Dawson and Jenny Colgan for the brilliant insight into every facet of *Mary Poppins* and letting me quote our conversations. And thanks to all those others who have responded to my tweets on the subject or got in touch with your own thoughts. All this has been invaluable.

Thanks to the team at Vivienne Clore Management for the support, encouragement and understanding.

Thanks to my family and friends, and especially my parents and my sister, who shared multiple viewings of *Mary Poppins* with me at an early age and are always so supportive of me in my endeavours. Thanks to my grandma, Violet, to whom I owe so much and who we lost in 2020. She is survived by her husband Geoffrey, also a force of nature, just as she was. This book is dedicated to her memory. She had a wonderfully Poppins energy.

Thanks to David, who never stops making this possible for me, and who is the greatest partner a writer could hope for. And thanks to Skye and Thomas who make everything seem worth it.

# Index

Blyton, Enid 17—18, 20, 150
Boom, Admiral 35, 36, 44, 48, 129, 134, 143, 173
Brand, Katy (KB)
    ancestral stock 83—4
    'anti-feminist' accusations 86
    'bowls of crap' 60
    and Brownies 18—19, 25—6
    button-sewing ability 25—6
    childhood stories 150—1
    cleaning job 60
    clothes and appearance, post-Poppins 66—8, 69—70
    clothes and appearance, pre-Poppins 22—3, 41, 65, 66
    comedy fashion show 18
    confidence around words 112
    conversation with young Peterson follower 140—1
    and Covid-19 lockdown 189—92
    distrust of financial sector 118—19
    dream to be Poppins in the house 63, 64
    evangelical church 79—80
    'Fame and Fortune' interview 123
    fantasy house 59, 60
    fear of post 24, 111
    flaws and weaknesses 11—4
    fondness for re-decorating 40
    freelance work and holidays 97—9
    and Girl Guides 19, 25
    hoarding instinct 39
    holidaying alone 96—7
    holidaying with reluctant ex-boyfriend 96
    hopelessness with money 111—12, 113—16, 123—4
    keeping things inside professionally 87—8
    likened to Poppins 21—2, 26
    literary heroines 17—18, 20
    love of brining order to the home 63
    love of laughing 19
    nanny fantasy 62—3
    need to address bad habits 24—6

# C

portrayal of witches 82
relationship with Travers 7, 93—4, 175—6, 182
and Travers' hostility to the Sherman Brothers 177—8
Disney Hall of Fame 172
Disneyland 8, 171, 183
Disney World 8, 38, 183
Dotrice, Karen 174—5, 181—2
*Dumbo* 170
Duncan, Isadora 173

## E

Edinburgh Festival 113, 115, 167
Ellen the maid 11, 83—4, 138
English Civil War 119

## F

'Feed the Birds' 46, 50
    Disney's favourite song 46, 121—2, 179—80
    triple interpretation 46, 121—2
Fellowes, Julian 11
feminism 26, 81, 85, 196
    second-wave 76, 184
'Fidelity Fiduciary Bank' 47, 120
film credits, at top of film 34—5
'follow your bliss' 153—4
Frances-White, Deborah 26
*Frozen* 82

## G

Garden of Eden 76
George (Famous Five) 17
Girl Guides 19, 25
God the Father 76
Grammys 176
*Guardian* 96

ONE PLACE. MANY STORIES

Bold, innovative and
empowering publishing.

FOLLOW US ON:

@HQStories